ON
CHRISTIANITY

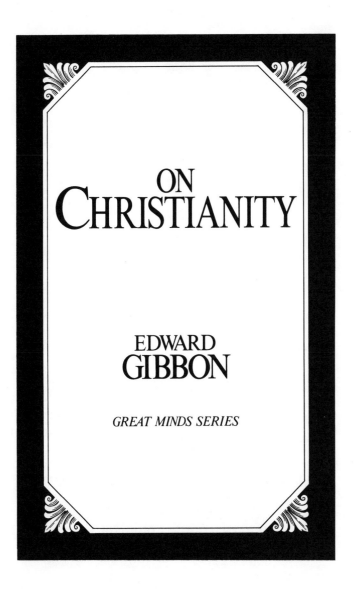

ON
CHRISTIANITY

EDWARD
GIBBON

GREAT MINDS SERIES

PROMETHEUS BOOKS
Buffalo, New York

Published 1991 by Prometheus Books

Editorial offices located at 700 East Amherst Street, Buffalo,
New York 14215, and distribution facilities at 59 John Glenn
Drive, Amherst, New York 14228

Library of Congress Catalog Number: 90-63887
ISBN 0-87975-674-8

Printed on acid-free paper in the United States of America

Also Available in Prometheus's Great Minds Paperback Series:

The Origin of Species
by Charles Darwin

EDWARD GIBBON was born, in comfortable circumstances, at Putney, Surrey, on April 27, 1737. As a child, Edward showed unusual precocity; but, because of a sickly constitution, he was kept mostly at home, where he devoured the contents of his grandfather's library. Gibbon matriculated at Magdalen College, Oxford, in 1752, but was removed by his father and, in the following year, placed under the tutelage of M. Pavillard, a Calvinist minister, in Lausanne, Switzerland. While at Lausanne, Gibbon mastered French and began a systematic study of the classics. It was also at this time that the future historian first formulated the religious philosophy to which he would adhere for the rest of his life: a moderate skepticism which, while accepting the existence of a deity, refused to claim any certainty about the precise workings of the divine will.

After leaving Lausanne in 1758, Gibbon did the gentleman's grand tour, arriving in Rome in 1764, where he first conceived the idea for his great history. Upon his return to England, Gibbon gained entrance to the fashionable and literary life of London, settling more or less permanently in the capital following the death of his father in 1770. In 1774, Gibbon secured a seat in Parliament, which he held for the next eight years, all the while working assiduously on his history.

The publication of the first volume of the *Decline and Fall of the Roman Empire* in 1776 made Gibbon immediately famous. The subsequent publication of volumes 2 through 6, between 1781 and 1788, secured forever his literary reputation. Adam Smith declared that the *Decline and Fall* set Gibbon "at the head of the whole literary tribe at present existing in Europe." Edward Gibbon died in London on January 16, 1794.

Gibbon's unfolding theme in *Decline and Fall* is that the destruction of the Roman Empire had been caused by both barbarism and Christianity. The fifteenth and sixteenth chapters of the historian's work, reprinted here, represent the first systematic and scholarly effort to reveal in a historial narrative the rise of Christianity as a natural process, not as the result of supernatural intervention.

Gibbon's forceful arguments, accepted by the unprejudiced and open-minded, were nonetheless attacked by contemporary theologians. But such attacks have not dimmed the reputation earned by a universally acknowledged master of historical narrative.

Edward Gibbon's other published works include *Essai sur l'étude de la littérature* (1761), *Critical Observations on the Sixth Book of the Aeneid* (1765), and *Vindication of Certain Passages* (1779).

GIBBON ON CHRISTIANITY

CHAPTER XV

THE PROGRESS OF THE CHRISTIAN RELIGION, AND THE
SENTIMENTS, MANNERS, NUMBERS, AND CONDITION
OF THE PRIMITIVE CHRISTIANS

A CANDID but rational inquiry into the progress and establishment of Christianity may be considered as a very essential part of the history of the Roman empire. While that great body was invaded by open violence, or undermined by slow decay, a pure and humble religion gently insinuated itself into the minds of men, grew up in silence and obscurity, derived new vigour from opposition, and finally erected the triumphant banner of the cross on the ruins of the Capitol. Nor was the influence of Christianity confined to the period or to the limits of the Roman empire. After a revolution of thirteen or fourteen centuries, that religion is still professed by the nations of Europe, the most distinguished portion of human kind in arts and learning as well as in arms. By the industry and zeal of the Europeans it has been widely diffused to the most distant shores of Asia and Africa; and by the means of their colonies has been firmly established from Canada to Chili, in a world unknown to the ancients.

But this inquiry, however useful or entertaining, is attended with two peculiar difficulties. The scanty and suspicious materials of ecclesiastical history seldom enable us to dispel the dark cloud that hangs over the first age of the church. The great law of impartiality too often obliges us to reveal the imperfections of the uninspired teachers and believers of the gospel; and, to a careless observer, *their* faults may seem to cast a shade on the faith which they professed. But the scandal of the pious Christian, and the fallacious triumph of the Infidel, should cease as soon as they recollect not only *by whom*, but likewise *to whom*, the Divine Revelation was given. The theologian may indulge the pleasing task of describing Religion as she descended from Heaven, arrayed in her native purity. A more melancholy duty is imposed on the historian. He must discover the inevitable mixture of error and corruption which she contracted in a long residence upon earth, among a weak and degenerate race of beings.

Our curiosity is naturally prompted to inquire by what means the Christian faith obtained so remarkable a victory over the established religions of the earth. To this inquiry an obvious but satisfactory answer may be returned: that it was owing to the convincing evidence of the doctrine itself, and to the ruling providence of its great Author. But, as truth and reason seldom find so favourable a reception in the world, and as the wisdom of Providence frequently condescends to use the passions of the human heart, and the general circumstances of mankind, as instruments to execute its purpose, we may still be permitted, though with becoming submission, to ask not indeed what were the first, but what were the secondary causes of the rapid growth of the Christian church. It will, perhaps, appear that it was most effectually favoured and assisted by the five following causes: I. The inflexible, and, if we may use the expression, the intolerant zeal of the Christians, derived, it is true, from the Jewish religion, but purified from the narrow and unsocial spirit which, instead of inviting, had deterred the Gentiles from embracing the law of Moses. II. The doctrine of a future life, improved by every additional circumstance which could give weight and efficacy to that important truth. III. The miraculous powers ascribed to the primitive church. IV. The pure and austere morals of the Christians. V. The union and discipline of the Christian republic, which gradually formed an independent and increasing state in the heart of the Roman empire.

I. We have already described the religious harmony of the ancient world, and the facility with which the most different and even hostile nations embraced, or at least respected, each other's superstitions. A single people refused to join in the common intercourse of mankind. The Jews, who, under the Assyrian and Persian monarchies, had languished for many ages the most despised portion of their slaves, emerged from obscurity under the successors of Alexander; and, as they multiplied to a surprising degree in the East, and afterwards in the West, they soon excited the curiosity and wonder of other nations. The sullen obstinacy with which they maintained their peculiar rites and unsocial manners seemed to mark them out a distinct species of men, who boldly professed, or who faintly disguised, their implacable hatred to the rest of human kind. Neither the violence of Antiochus, nor the arts of Herod, nor the example of the circumjacent nations, could ever persuade the Jews to associate with the institutions of Moses the elegant mythology of the Greeks. According to the maxims of universal toleration, the Romans protected a superstition which they despised. The polite Augustus condescended to give orders that sacrifices should be offered for his prosperity in the temple of Jerusalem; while the meanest of the posterity of Abraham, who should have paid the same homage to the Jupiter of the Capitol, would have been an object of abhorrence to himself and to his brethren. But the moderation of the conquerors was insufficient to appease the jealous prejudices of their subjects, who were alarmed and scandalized at the ensigns of paganism, which necessarily introduced themselves into a Roman province. The mad attempt of Caligula to place his own statue in the temple of Jerusalem was defeated by the unanimous resolution of a people who dreaded death much less than such an idolatrous profanation. Their attachment to the law of Moses was equal to their detestation of foreign religions. The current of zeal and devotion, as it was contracted into a narrow channel, ran with the strength, and sometimes with the fury, of a torrent.

This inflexible perseverance, which appeared so odious, or so ridiculous, to the ancient world, assumes a more awful character, since Providence has deigned to reveal to us the mysterious history of the chosen people. But the devout, and even scrupulous, attachment to the Mosaic religion, so conspicuous among the Jews who lived under the second temple, becomes still more surprising if it is compared with the stubborn incredulity of their forefathers. When the law was given in thunder from Mount Sinai; when the tides of the ocean and the course of the planets were suspended for the convenience of the Israelites; and when temporal rewards and punishments were the immediate consequences of their piety or disobedience, they perpetually relapsed into rebellion against the visible majesty of their Divine King, placed the idols of the nations in the sanctuary of Jehovah, and imitated every fantastic ceremony that was practised in the tents of the Arabs or in the cities of Phœnicia. As the protection of Heaven was deservedly withdrawn from the ungrateful race, their faith acquired a proportionable degree of vigour and purity. The contemporaries of Moses and Joshua had beheld, with careless indifference, the most amazing miracles. Under the pressure of every calamity, the belief of those miracles has preserved the Jews of a later period from the universal contagion of idolatry; and, in contradiction to every known principle of the human mind, that singular people seems to have yielded a stronger and more ready assent to the traditions of their remote ancestors than to the evidence of their own senses.

The Jewish religion was admirably fitted for defence, but it was never designed for conquest; and it seems probable that the number of proselytes was never much superior to that of apostates. The divine promises were originally made, and the distinguishing rite of circumcision was enjoined, to a single family. When the posterity of Abraham had multiplied like the sands of the sea, the Deity, from whose mouth they received a system of laws and ceremonies, declared himself the proper and, as it were, the national God of Israel; and, with the most jealous care, separated his favourite people from the rest of mankind. The conquest of the land of Canaan was accompanied with so many wonderful and with so many bloody circumstances that the victorious Jews were left in a state of irreconcilable hostility with all their neighbours. They had been commanded to extirpate some of the most idolatrous tribes; and the execution of the Divine will had seldom been retarded by the weakness of humanity. With the other nations they were forbidden to contract any marriages or alliances; and the prohibition of receiving them into the congregation, which in some cases was perpetual, almost always extended to the third, to the seventh, or even to the tenth generation. The obligation of preaching to the Gentiles the faith of Moses had never been inculcated as a precept of the law, nor were the Jews inclined to impose it on themselves as a voluntary duty. In the admission of new citizens, that unsocial people was actuated by the selfish vanity of the Greeks, rather than by the generous policy of Rome. The descendants of Abraham were flattered by the opinion that they alone were the heirs of the covenant; and they were apprehensive of diminishing the value of their inheritance by sharing it too easily with the strangers of the earth. A larger acquaintance with mankind extended their knowledge without correcting their prejudices; and, whenever the God of Israel acquired any new votaries, he was much more indebted to the inconstant humour of polytheism than to the active zeal of his own missionaries. The religion of Moses seems to be instituted for a particular country, as well as for a single nation; and, if a strict obedience had been paid to the order that every male, three times in the year, should present himself before the Lord Jehovah, it would have been impossible that the Jews could ever have spread themselves beyond the narrow limits of the promised land. That obstacle was indeed removed by the destruction of the temple of Jerusalem; but the most considerable part of the Jewish religion was involved in its destruction; and the Pagans, who had long wondered at the strange

report of an empty sanctuary, were at a loss to discover what could be the object, or what could be the
instruments, of a worship which was destitute of
temples and of altars, of priests and of sacrifices. Yet
even in their fallen state the Jews, still asserting
their lofty and exclusive privileges, shunned instead
of courting the society of strangers. They still
insisted with inflexible rigour on those parts of the
law which it was in their power to practise. Their
peculiar distinctions of days, of meats, and a variety
of trivial though burdensome observances, were so
many objects of disgust and aversion for the other
nations, to whose habits and prejudices they were
diametrically opposite. The painful and even dangerous rite of circumcision was alone capable of repelling
a willing proselyte from the door of the synagogue.

Under these circumstances, Christianity offered
itself to the world, armed with the strength of the
Mosaic law, and delivered from the weight of its
fetters. An exclusive zeal for the truth of religion
and the unity of God was as carefully inculcated in the
new as in the ancient system; and whatever was now
revealed to mankind, concerning the nature and
designs of the Supreme Being, was fitted to increase
their reverence for that mysterious doctrine. The
divine authority of Moses and the prophets was
admitted, and even established, as the firmest basis
of Christianity. From the beginning of the world, an
uninterrupted series of predictions had announced
and prepared the long expected coming of the Messiah,
who, in compliance with the gross apprehensions of
the Jews, had been more frequently represented under
the character of a King and Conqueror than under
that of a Prophet, a Martyr, and the Son of God.
By his expiatory sacrifice, the imperfect sacrifices
of the temple were at once consummated and abolished.
The ceremonial law, which consisted only of types and
figures, was succeeded by a pure and spiritual worship,
equally adapted to all climates, as well as to every
condition of mankind; and to the initiation of blood
was substituted a more harmless initiation of water.

The promise of divine favour, instead of being partially confined to the posterity of Abraham, was universally proposed to the freeman and the slave, to the Greek and to the barbarian, to the Jew and to the Gentile. Every privilege that could raise the proselyte from earth to Heaven, that could exalt his devotion, secure his happiness, or even gratify that secret pride which, under the semblance of devotion, insinuates itself into the human heart, was still reserved for the members of the Christian church; but at the same time all mankind was permitted, and even solicited, to accept the glorious distinction, which was not only proffered as a favour, but imposed as an obligation. It became the most sacred duty of a new convert to diffuse among his friends and relations the inestimable blessing which he had received, and to warn them against a refusal that would be severely punished as a criminal disobedience to the will of a benevolent but all-powerful deity.

The enfranchisement of the church from the bonds of the synagogue was a work however of some time and of some difficulty. The Jewish converts, who acknowledged Jesus in the character of the Messiah foretold by their ancient oracles, respected him as a prophetic teacher of virtue and religion; but they obstinately adhered to the ceremonies of their ancestors, and were desirous of imposing them on the Gentiles, who continually augmented the number of believers. These Judaizing Christians seem to have argued with some degree of plausibility from the divine origin of the Mosaic law, and from the immutable perfections of its great Author. They affirmed *that*, if the Being, who is the same through all eternity, had designed to abolish those sacred rites which had served to distinguish his chosen people, the repeal of them would have been no less clear and solemn than their first promulgation: *that*, instead of those frequent declarations, which either suppose or assert the perpetuity of the Mosaic religion, it would have been represented as a provisionary scheme intended to last only till the coming of the Messiah, who should instruct mankind in a more perfect mode of faith and

of worship : *that* the Messiah himself, and his disciples
who conversed with him on earth, instead of authoris-
ing by their example the most minute observances of
the Mosaic law, would have published to the world the
abolition of those useless and obsolete ceremonies,
without suffering Christianity to remain during so
many years obscurely confounded among the sects of
the Jewish church.   Arguments like these appear to
have been used in the defence of the expiring cause of
the Mosaic law; but the industry of our learned
divines has abundantly explained the ambiguous
language of the Old Testament, and the ambiguous
conduct of the apostolic teachers.   It was proper
gradually to unfold the system of the Gospel, and to
pronounce, with the utmost caution and tenderness,
a sentence of condemnation so repugnant to the
inclination and prejudices of the believing Jews.

The history of the church of Jerusalem affords a
lively proof of the necessity of those precautions, and
of the deep impression which the Jewish religion had
made on the minds of its sectaries.   The first fifteen
bishops of Jerusalem were all circumcised Jews; and
the congregation over which they presided united the
law of Moses with the doctrine of Christ.   It was
natural that the primitive tradition of a church which
was founded only forty years after the death of Christ,
and was governed almost as many years under the
immediate inspection of his apostle, should be received
as the standard of orthodoxy.   The distant churches
very frequently appealed to the authority of their
venerable Parent, and relieved her distress by a liberal
contribution of alms.   But when numerous and
opulent societies were established in the great cities of
the empire, in Antioch, Alexandria, Ephesus, Corinth,
and Rome, the reverence which Jerusalem had
inspired to all the Christian colonies insensibly
diminished.   The Jewish converts, or, as they were
afterwards called, the Nazarenes, who had laid the
foundations of the church, soon found themselves
overwhelmed by the increasing multitudes that from
all the various religions of polytheism inlisted under

the banner of Christ; and the Gentiles, who with the approbation of their peculiar apostle had rejected the intolerable weight of Mosaic ceremonies, at length refused to their more scrupulous brethren the same toleration which at first they had humbly solicited for their own practice. The ruin of the temple, of the city, and of the public religion of the Jews, was severely felt by the Nazarenes; as in their manners, though not in their faith, they maintained so intimate a connexion with their impious countrymen, whose misfortunes were attributed by the Pagans to the contempt, and more justly ascribed by the Christians to the wrath, of the Supreme Deity. The Nazarenes retired from the ruins of Jerusalem to the little town of Pella beyond the Jordan, where that ancient church languished above sixty years in solitude and obscurity. They still enjoyed the comfort of making frequent and devout visits to the *Holy City*, and the hope of being one day restored to those seats which both nature and religion taught them to love as well as to revere. But at length, under the reign of Hadrian, the desperate fanaticism of the Jews filled up the measure of their calamities; and the Romans, exasperated by their repeated rebellions, exercised the rights of victory with unusual rigour. The emperor founded, under the name of Ælia Capitolina, a new city on Mount Sion, to which he gave the privileges of a colony; and, denouncing the severest penalties against any of the Jewish people who should dare to approach its precincts, he fixed a vigilant garrison of a Roman cohort to enforce the execution of his orders. The Nazarenes had only one way left to escape the common proscription, and the force of truth was on this occasion assisted by the influence of temporal advantages. They elected Marcus for their bishop, a prelate of the race of the Gentiles, and most probably a native either of Italy or of some of the Latin provinces. At his persuasion the most considerable part of the congregation renounced the Mosaic law, in the practice of which they had persevered above a century. By this sacrifice of their habits and prejudices they purchased a free admission into the colony of Hadrian, and more firmly cemented their union with the Catholic church.

When the name and honours of the church of Jerusalem had been restored to Mount Sion, the crimes of heresy and schism were imputed to the obscure remnant of the Nazarenes which refused to accompany their Latin bishop. They still preserved their former habitation of Pella, spread themselves into the villages adjacent to Damascus, and formed an inconsiderable church in the city of Berœa, or, as it is now called, of Aleppo, in Syria. The name of Nazarenes was deemed too honourable for those Christian Jews, and they soon received, from the supposed poverty of their understanding as well as of their condition, the contemptuous epithet of Ebionites. In a few years after the return of the church of Jerusalem, it became a matter of doubt and controversy whether a man who sincerely acknowledged Jesus as the Messiah, but who still continued to observe the law of Moses, could possibly hope for salvation. The humane temper of Justin Martyr inclined him to answer this question in the affirmative; and, though he expressed himself with the most guarded diffidence, he ventured to determine in favour of such an imperfect Christian, if he were content to practise the Mosaic ceremonies, without pretending to assert their general use or necessity. But when Justin was pressed to declare the sentiment of the church, he confessed that there were very many among the orthodox Christians who not only excluded their Judaizing brethren from the hope of salvation, but who declined any intercourse with them in the common offices of friendship, hospitality, and social life. The more rigorous opinion prevailed, as it was natural to expect, over the milder; and an external bar of separation was fixed between the disciples of Moses and those of Christ. The unfortunate Ebionites, rejected from one religion as apostates, and from the other as heretics, found themselves compelled to assume a more decided character; and, although some traces of that obsolete sect may be discovered as late as the fourth century, they insensibly melted away either into the church or the synagogue.

While the orthodox church preserved a just medium between excessive veneration and improper contempt for the law of Moses, the various heretics deviated into equal but opposite extremes of error and extravagance. From the acknowledged truth of the Jewish religion the Ebionites had concluded that it could never be abolished. From its supposed imperfections the Gnostics as hastily inferred that it never was instituted by the wisdom of the Deity. There are some objections against the authority of Moses and the prophets which too readily present themselves to the sceptical mind, though they can only be derived from our ignorance of remote antiquity and from our incapacity to form an adequate judgment of the divine œconomy. These objections were eagerly embraced, and as petulantly urged, by the vain science of the Gnostics. As those heretics were, for the most part, averse to the pleasures of sense, they morosely arraigned the polygamy of the patriarchs, the gallantries of David, and the seraglio of Solomon. The conquest of the land of Canaan, and the extirpation of the unsuspecting natives, they were at a loss how to reconcile with the common notions of humanity and justice. But, when they recollected the sanguinary list of murders, of executions, and of massacres, which stain almost every page of the Jewish annals, they acknowledged that the barbarians of Palestine had exercised as much compassion towards their idolatrous enemies as they had ever shewn to their friends or countrymen. Passing from the sectaries of the law to the law itself, they asserted that it was impossible that a religion which consisted only of bloody sacrifices and trifling ceremonies, and whose rewards as well as punishments were all of a carnal and temporal nature, could inspire the love of virtue, or restrain the impetuosity of passion. The Mosaic account of the creation and fall of man was treated with profane derision by the Gnostics, who would not listen with patience to the repose of the Deity after six days' labour, to the rib of Adam, the garden of Eden, the trees of life and of knowledge, the speaking serpent, the forbidden fruit, and the condemnation pronounced against human kind for the venial offence of their first progenitors. The God of Israel was impiously represented by the Gnostics as a being liable to passion and to error, capricious in his favour, implacable in his resentment, meanly jealous of his superstitious worship, and confining his partial providence to a single people and to this transitory life.   In such a character they could discover none of the features of the wise and omnipotent father of the universe.   They allowed that the religion of the Jews was somewhat less criminal than the idolatry of the Gentiles; but it was their fundamental doctrine that the Christ whom they adored as the first and brightest emanation of the Deity appeared upon earth to rescue mankind from their various errors, and to reveal a *new* system of truth and perfection.   The most learned of the fathers, by a very singular condescension, have imprudently admitted the sophistry of the Gnostics. Acknowledging that the literal sense is repugnant to every principle of faith as well as reason, they deem themselves secure and invulnerable behind the ample veil of allegory, which they carefully spread over every tender part of the Mosaic dispensation.

It has been remarked, with more ingenuity than truth, that the virgin purity of the church was never violated by schism or heresy before the reign of Trajan or Hadrian, about one hundred years after the death of Christ.   We may observe, with much more propriety, that during that period the disciples of the Messiah were indulged in a freer latitude both of faith and practice than has ever been allowed in succeeding ages.   As the terms of communion were insensibly narrowed, and the spiritual authority of the prevailing party was exercised with increasing severity, many of its most respectable adherents, who were called upon to renounce, were provoked to assert, their private opinions, to pursue the consequences of their mistaken principles, and openly to erect the standard of rebellion against the unity of the church. The Gnostics were distinguished as the most polite, the most learned, and the most wealthy of the Christian name, and that general appellation which expressed a superiority of knowledge was either assumed by their own pride or ironically bestowed by the envy of their adversaries. They were almost without exception of the race of the Gentiles, and their principal founders seem to have been natives of Syria or Egypt, where the warmth of the climate disposes both the mind and the body to indolent and contemplative devotion. The Gnostics blended with the faith of Christ many sublime but obscure tenets which they derived from oriental philosophy, and even from the religion of Zoroaster, concerning the eternity of matter, the existence of two principles, and the mysterious hierarchy of the invisible world. As soon as they launched out into that vast abyss, they delivered themselves to the guidance of a disordered imagination; and, as the paths of error are various and infinite, the Gnostics were imperceptibly divided into more than fifty particular sects, of whom the most celebrated appear to have been the Basilidians, the Valentinians, the Marcionites, and, in a still later period, the Manichæans. Each of these sects could boast of its bishops and congregations, of its doctors and martyrs, and, instead of the four gospels adopted by the church, the heretics produced a multitude of histories, in which the actions and discourses of Christ and of his apostles were adapted to their respective tenets. The success of the Gnostics was rapid and extensive. They covered Asia and Egypt, established themselves in Rome, and sometimes penetrated into the provinces of the West. For the most part they arose in the second century, flourished during the third, and were suppressed in the fourth or fifth, by the prevalence of more fashionable controversies, and by the superior ascendant of the reigning power. Though they constantly disturbed the peace, and frequently disgraced the name, of religion, they contributed to assist rather than to retard the progress of Christianity. The Gentile converts, whose strongest objections and prejudices were directed against the law of Moses, could find admission into many Christian societies, which required not from their untutored mind any belief of an antecedent revelation. Their faith was insensibly fortified and enlarged, and the church was ultimately benefited by the conquests of its most inveterate enemies.

But, whatever difference of opinion might subsist between the Orthodox, the Ebionites, and the Gnostics, concerning the divinity or the obligation of the Mosaic law, they were all equally animated by the same exclusive zeal and by the same abhorrence for idolatry which had distinguished the Jews from the other nations of the ancient world. The philosopher, who considered the system of polytheism as a composition of human fraud and error, could disguise a smile of contempt under the mask of devotion, without apprehending that either the mockery or the compliance would expose him to the resentment of any invisible, or, as he conceived them, imaginary powers. But the established religions of Paganism were seen by the primitive Christians in a much more odious and formidable light. It was the universal sentiment both of the church and of heretics that the dæmons were the authors, the patrons, and the objects of idolatry. Those rebellious spirits who had been degraded from the rank of angels, and cast down into the infernal pit, were still permitted to roam upon earth, to torment the bodies, and to seduce the minds, of sinful men. The dæmons soon discovered and abused the natural propensity of the human heart towards devotion, and, artfully withdrawing the adoration of mankind from their Creator, they usurped the place and honours of the Supreme Deity. By the success of their malicious contrivances, they at once gratified their own vanity and revenge, and obtained the only comfort of which they were yet susceptible, the hope of involving the human species in the participation of their guilt and misery. It was confessed, or at least it was imagined, that they had distributed among themselves the most important characters of polytheism, one dæmon assuming the name and attributes of Jupiter, another of Æsculapius, a third of Venus, and a fourth perhaps of Apollo; and that, by the advantage of their long experience and aerial nature, they were enabled to execute, with sufficient skill and dignity, the parts which they had undertaken. They lurked in the temples, instituted festivals and sacrifices, invented fables, pronounced oracles, and were frequently allowed to perform miracles. The Christians, who, by the interposition of evil spirits, could so readily explain every præternatural appearance, were disposed and even desirous to admit the most extravagant fictions of the Pagan mythology. But the belief of the Christian was accompanied with horror. The most trifling mark of respect to the national worship he considered as a direct homage yielded to the dæmon, and as an act of rebellion against the majesty of God.

In consequence of this opinion, it was the first but arduous duty of a Christian to preserve himself pure and undefiled by the practice of idolatry. The religion of the nations was not merely a speculative doctrine professed in the schools or preached in the temples. The innumerable deities and rites of polytheism were closely interwoven with every circumstance of business or pleasure, of public or of private life; and it seemed impossible to escape the observance of them without at the same time renouncing the commerce of mankind and all the offices and amusements of society. The important transactions of peace and war were prepared or concluded by solemn sacrifices, in which the magistrate, the senator, and the soldier were obliged to preside or to participate. The public spectacles were an essential part of the cheerful devotion of the Pagans, and the gods were supposed to accept, as the most grateful offering, the games that the prince and people celebrated in honour of their peculiar festivals. The Christian, who with pious horror avoided the abomination of the circus or the theatre, found himself encompassed with infernal snares in every convivial entertainment, as often as his friends, invoking the hospitable deities, poured out libations to each other's happiness. When the bride, struggling with well-affected reluctance, was forced in hymenæal pomp over the threshold of her new habitation, or when the sad procession of the dead slowly moved towards the funeral pile, the Christian, on these interesting occasions, was compelled to desert the persons who were the dearest to him rather than contract the guilt inherent to those impious ceremonies. Every art and every trade that was in the least concerned in the framing or adorning of idols was polluted by the stain of idolatry; a severe sentence, since it devoted to eternal misery the far greater part of the community, which is employed in the exercise of liberal or mechanic professions. If we cast our eyes over the numerous remains of antiquity, we shall perceive that, besides the immediate representations of the Gods and the holy instruments of their worship, the elegant forms and agreeable fictions consecrated by the imagination of the Greeks were introduced as the richest ornaments of the houses, the dress, and the furniture, of the Pagans. Even the arts of music and painting, of eloquence and poetry, flowed from the same impure origin. In the style of the fathers, Apollo and the Muses were the organs of the infernal spirit, Homer and Virgil were the most eminent of his servants, and the beautiful mythology which pervades and animates the compositions of their genius is destined to celebrate the glory of the dæmons. Even the common language of Greece and Rome abounded with familiar but impious expressions, which the imprudent Christian might too carelessly utter, or too patiently hear.

The dangerous temptations which on every side lurked in ambush to surprise the unguarded believer assailed him with redoubled violence on the days of solemn festivals. So artfully were they framed and disposed throughout the year that superstition always wore the appearance of pleasure, and often of virtue. Some of the most sacred festivals in the Roman ritual were destined to salute the new calends of January with vows of public and private felicity, to indulge the pious remembrance of the dead and living, to ascertain the inviolable bounds of property, to hail, on the return of spring, the genial powers of fecundity, to perpetuate the two memorable æras of Rome, the foundation of the city and that of the republic, and to restore, during the humane license of the Saturnalia, the primitive equality of mankind. Some idea may be conceived of the abhorrence of the Christians for such impious ceremonies, by the scrupulous delicacy which they displayed on a much less alarming occasion. On days of general festivity, it was the custom of the ancients to adorn their doors with lamps and with branches of laurel, and to crown their heads with a garland of flowers. This innocent and elegant practice might, perhaps, have been tolerated as a mere civil institution. But it most unluckily happened that the doors were under the protection of the household gods, that the laurel was sacred to the lover of Daphne, and that garlands of flowers, though frequently worn as a symbol either of joy or mourning, had been dedicated in their first origin to the service of superstition. The trembling Christians, who were persuaded in this instance to comply with the fashion of their country and the commands of the magistrate, laboured under the most gloomy apprehensions, from the reproaches of their own conscience, the censures of the church, and the denunciations of divine vengeance.

Such was the anxious diligence which was required to guard the chastity of the gospel from the infectious breath of idolatry. The superstitious observances of public or private rites were carelessly practised, from education and habit, by the followers of the established religion. But as often as they occurred they afforded the Christians an opportunity of declaring and confirming their zealous opposition. By these frequent protestations their attachment to the faith was continually fortified, and in proportion to the increase of zeal they combated with the more ardour and success in the holy war which they had undertaken against the empire of the dæmons.

II. The writings of Cicero represent, in the most lively colours, the ignorance, the errors, and the uncertainty of the ancient philosophers with regard to the immortality of the soul. When they are desirous of arming their disciples against the fear of death, they inculcate, as an obvious though melancholy position, that the fatal stroke of our dissolution releases us from the calamities of life, and that those can no longer suffer who no longer exist. Yet there were a few sages of Greece and Rome who had conceived a more exalted, and, in some respects, a juster idea of human nature; though it must be confessed that, in the sublime inquiry, their reason had been often guided by their imagination, and that their imagination had been prompted by their vanity. When they viewed with complacency the extent of their own mental powers, when they exercised the various faculties of memory, of fancy, and of judgment, in the most profound speculations, or the most important labours, and when they reflected on the desire of fame, which transported them into future ages far beyond the bounds of death and of the grave, they were unwilling to confound themselves with the beasts of the field, or to suppose that a being, for whose dignity they entertained the most sincere admiration, could be limited to a spot of earth, and to a few years of duration. With this favourable prepossession, they summoned to their aid the science, or rather the language, of Metaphysics. They soon discovered that, as none of the properties of matter will apply to the operations of the mind, the human soul must consequently be a substance distinct from the body, pure, simple, and spiritual, incapable of dissolution, and susceptible of a much higher degree of virtue and happiness after the release from its corporeal prison. From these spacious and noble principles, the philosophers who trod in the footsteps of Plato deduced a very unjustifiable conclusion, since they asserted, not only the future immortality, but the past eternity of the human soul, which they were too apt to consider as a portion of the infinite and self-existing spirit which pervades and sustains the universe. A doctrine thus removed beyond the senses and the experience of mankind might serve to amuse the leisure of a philosophic mind; or, in the silence of solitude, it might sometimes impart a ray of comfort to desponding virtue; but the faint impression which had been received in the schools was soon obliterated by the commerce and business of active life. We are sufficiently acquainted with the eminent persons who flourished in the age of Cicero, and of the first Cæsars, with their actions, their characters, and their motives, to be assured that their conduct in this life was never regulated by any serious conviction of the rewards or punishments of a future state. At the bar and in the senate of Rome the ablest orators were not apprehensive of giving offence to their hearers by exposing that doctrine as an idle and extravagant opinion, which was rejected with contempt by every man of a liberal education and understanding.

Since, therefore, the most sublime efforts of philosophy can extend no farther than feebly to point out the desire, the hope, or at most the probability, of a future state, there is nothing, except a divine revelation, that can ascertain the existence, and describe the condition, of the invisible country which is destined to receive the souls of men after their separation from the body. But we may perceive several defects inherent to the popular religions of Greece and Rome, which rendered them very unequal to so arduous a task. 1. The general system of their mythology was unsupported by any solid proofs; and the wisest among the Pagans had already disclaimed its usurped authority. 2. The description of the infernal regions had been abandoned to the fancy of painters and of poets, who peopled them with so many phantoms and monsters, who dispensed their rewards and punishments with so little equity, that a solemn truth, the most congenial to the human heart, was oppressed and disgraced by the absurd mixture of the wildest fictions. 3. The doctrine of a future state was scarcely considered among the devout polytheists of

Greece and Rome as a fundamental article of faith. The providence of the gods, as it related to public communities rather than to private individuals, was principally displayed on the visible theatre of the present world. The petitions which were offered on the altars of Jupiter or Apollo expressed the anxiety of their worshippers for temporal happiness, and their ignorance or indifference concerning a future life. The important truth of the immortality of the soul was inculcated with more diligence as well as success in India, in Assyria, in Egypt, and in Gaul; and, since we cannot attribute such a difference to the superior knowledge of the barbarians, we must ascribe it to the influence of an established priesthood, which employed the motives of virtue as the instrument of ambition.

We might naturally expect that a principle so essential to religion would have been revealed in the clearest terms to the chosen people of Palestine, and that it might safely have been intrusted to the hereditary priesthood of Aaron. It is incumbent on us to adore the mysterious dispensations of Providence when we discover that the doctrine of the immortality of the soul is omitted in the law of Moses; it is darkly insinuated by the prophets, and during the long period which elapsed between the Egyptian and the Babylonian servitudes, the hopes as well as fears of the Jews appear to have been confined within the narrow compass of the present life. After Cyrus had permitted the exiled nation to return into the promised land, and after Ezra had restored the ancient records of their religion, two celebrated sects, the Sadducees and the Pharisees, insensibly arose at Jerusalem. The former, selected from the more opulent and distinguished ranks of society, were strictly attached to the literal sense of the Mosaic law, and they piously rejected the immortality of the soul, as an opinion that received no countenance from the Divine book, which they revered as the only rule of their faith. To the authority of scripture the Pharisees added that of tradition, and they accepted, under the name of traditions, several speculative tenets from the philosophy or religion of the eastern nations. The doctrines of fate or predestination, of angels and spirits, and of a future state of rewards and punishments, were in the number of these new articles of belief; and as the Pharisees by the austerity of their manners, had drawn into their party the body of the Jewish people, the immortality of the soul became the prevailing sentiment of the synagogue, under the reign of the Asmonæan princes and pontiffs. The temper of the Jews was incapable of contenting itself with such a cold and languid assent as might satisfy the mind of a Polytheist; and as soon as they admitted the idea of a future state they embraced it with the zeal which has always formed the characteristic of the nation. Their zeal, however, added nothing to its evidence, or even probability; and it was still necessary that the doctrine of life and immortality, which had been dictated by nature, approved by reason, and received by superstition, should obtain the sanction of Divine truth from the authority and example of Christ.

When the promise of eternal happiness was proposed to mankind, on condition of adopting the faith and of observing the precepts of the gospel, it is no wonder that so advantageous an offer should have been accepted by great numbers of every religion, of every rank, and of every province in the Roman empire. The ancient Christians were animated by a contempt for their present existence, and by a just confidence of immortality, of which the doubtful and imperfect faith of modern ages cannot give us any adequate notion. In the primitive church, the influence of truth was very powerfully strengthened by an opinion which, however it may deserve respect for its usefulness and antiquity, has not been found agreeable to experience. It was universally believed that the end of the world and the kingdom of Heaven were at hand. The near approach of this wonderful event had been predicted by the apostles; the tradition of it was preserved by their earliest disciples, and those who understood in their literal sense the discourses of

Christ himself were obliged to expect the second and glorious coming of the Son of Man in the clouds, before that generation was totally extinguished which had beheld his humble condition upon earth, and which might still be witness of the calamities of the Jews under Vespasian or Hadrian. The revolution of seventeen centuries has instructed us not to press too closely the mysterious language of prophecy and revelation; but as long as, for wise purposes, this error was permitted to subsist in the church, it was productive of the most salutary effects on the faith and practice of Christians, who lived in the awful expectation of that moment when the globe itself, and all the various race of mankind, should tremble at the appearance of their divine judge.

The ancient and popular doctrine of the Millennium was intimately connected with the second coming of Christ. As the works of the creation had been finished in six days, their duration in their present state, according to a tradition which was attributed to the prophet Elijah, was fixed to six thousand years. By the same analogy it was inferred that this long period of labour and contention, which was now almost elapsed, would be succeeded by a joyful Sabbath of a thousand years; and that Christ, with the triumphant band of the saints and the elect who had escaped death, or who had been miraculously revived, would reign upon earth till the time appointed for the last and general resurrection. So pleasing was this hope to the mind of believers that the *New Jerusalem*, the seat of this blissful kingdom, was quickly adorned with all the gayest colours of the imagination. A felicity consisting only of pure and spiritual pleasure would have appeared too refined for its inhabitants, who were still supposed to possess their human nature and senses. A garden of Eden, with the amusements of the pastoral life, was no longer suited to the advanced state of society which prevailed under the Roman empire. A city was therefore erected of gold and precious stones, and a supernatural plenty of corn and wine was bestowed

on the adjacent territory; in the free enjoyment of
whose spontaneous productions the happy and
benevolent people was never to be restrained by any
jealous laws of exclusive property.   The assurance of
such a Millennium was carefully inculcated by a
succession of fathers from Justin Martyr and Irenæus,
who conversed with the immediate disciples of the
apostles, down to Lactantius, who was preceptor to
the son of Constantine. Though it might not be
universally received, it appears to have been the
reigning sentiment of the orthodox believers; and it
seems so well adapted to the desires and apprehensions of mankind that it must have contributed,
in a very considerable degree, to the progress of the
Christian faith.   But, when the edifice of the church
was almost completed, the temporary support was
laid aside.   The doctrine of Christ's reign upon earth
was at first treated as a profound allegory, was considered by degrees as a doubtful and useless opinion,
and was at length rejected as the absurd invention
of heresy and fanaticism.   A mysterious prophecy,
which still forms a part of the sacred canon, but which
was thought to favour the exploded sentiment, has
very narrowly escaped the proscription of the church.
   Whilst the happiness and glory of a temporal reign
were promised to the disciples of Christ, the most
dreadful calamities were denounced against an unbelieving world.   The edification of the new Jerusalem
was to advance by equal steps with the destruction of
the mystic Babylon; and, as long as the emperors
who reigned before Constantine persisted in the profession of idolatry, the epithet of Babylon was applied
to the city and to the empire of Rome.   A regular
series was prepared of all the moral and physical evils
which can afflict a flourishing nation; intestine discord, and the invasion of the fiercest barbarians from
the unknown regions of the North; pestilence and
famine, comets and eclipses, earthquakes and inunda-
tions.   All these were only so many preparatory and
alarming signs of the great catastrophe of Rome,
when the country of the Scipios and Cæsars should be

consumed by a flame from Heaven, and the city of the seven hills, with her palaces, her temples, and her triumphal arches, should be buried in a vast lake of fire and brimstone. It might, however, afford some consolation to Roman vanity, that the period of their empire would be that of the world itself; which, as it had once perished by the element of water, was destined to experience a second and a speedy destruction from the element of fire. In the opinion of a general conflagration, the faith of the Christian very happily coincided with the tradition of the East, the philosophy of the Stoics, and the analogy of Nature; and even the country which, from religious motives, had been chosen for the origin and principal scene of the conflagration, was the best adapted for that purpose by natural and physical causes; by its deep caverns, beds of sulphur, and numerous volcanoes, of which those of Ætna, of Vesuvius, and of Lipari, exhibit a very imperfect representation. The calmest and most intrepid sceptic could not refuse to acknowledge that the destruction of the present system of the world by fire was in itself extremely probable. The Christian, who founded his belief much less on the fallacious arguments of reason than on the authority of tradition and the interpretation of scripture, expected it with terror and confidence, as a certain and approaching event; and, as his mind was perpetually filled with the solemn idea, he considered every disaster that happened to the empire as an infallible symptom of an expiring world.

The condemnation of the wisest and most virtuous of the Pagans, on account of their ignorance or disbelief of the divine truth, seems to offend the reason and the humanity of the present age. But the primitive church, whose faith was of a much firmer consistence, delivered over, without hesitation, to eternal torture the far greater part of the human species. A charitable hope might perhaps be indulged in favour of Socrates, or some other sages of antiquity, who had consulted the light of reason before that of the gospel had arisen. But it was unanimously affirmed that those who, since the birth or the death of Christ, had obstinately persisted in the worship of the dæmons, neither deserved nor could expect a pardon from the irritated justice of the Deity. These rigid sentiments, which had been unknown to the ancient world, appear to have infused a spirit of bitterness into a system of love and harmony. The ties of blood and friendship were frequently torn asunder by the difference of religious faith; and the Christians, who in this world found themselves oppressed by the power of the Pagans, were sometimes seduced by resentment and spiritual pride to delight in the prospect of their future triumph. " You are fond of spectacles," exclaims the stern Tertullian; " expect the greatest of all spectacles, the last and eternal judgment of the universe. How shall I admire, how laugh, how rejoice, how exult, when I behold so many proud monarchs, and fancied gods, groaning in the lowest abyss of darkness; so many magistrates, who persecuted the name of the Lord, liquefying in fiercer fires than they ever kindled against the Christians; so many sage philosophers blushing in red hot flames, with their deluded scholars; so many celebrated poets trembling before the tribunal, not of Minos, but of Christ; so many tragedians, more tuneful in the expression of their own sufferings; so many dancers—— ! " But the humanity of the reader will permit me to draw a veil over the rest of this infernal description, which the zealous African pursues in a long variety of affected and unfeeling witticisms.

Doubtless there were many among the primitive Christians of a temper more suitable to the meekness and charity of their profession. There were many who felt a sincere compassion for the danger of their friends and countrymen, and who exerted the most benevolent zeal to save them from the impending destruction. The careless Polytheist, assailed by new and unexpected terrors, against which neither his priests nor his philosophers could afford him any certain protection, was very frequently terrified and subdued by the menace of eternal tortures. His fears might assist the progress of his faith and reason; and, if he could once persuade himself to suspect that the Christian religion might possibly be true, it became an easy task to convince him that it was the safest and most prudent party that he could possibly embrace,

III. The supernatural gifts which even in this life were ascribed to the Christians above the rest of mankind must have conduced to their own comfort, and very frequently to the conviction of infidels. Besides the occasional prodigies, which might sometimes be effected by the immediate interposition of the Deity when he suspended the laws of Nature for the service of religion, the Christian church, from the time of the apostles and their first disciples, has claimed an uninterrupted succession of miraculous powers, the gift of tongues, of vision and of prophecy, the power of expelling dæmons, of healing the sick, and of raising the dead. The knowledge of foreign languages was frequently communicated to the contemporaries of Irenæus, though Irenæus himself was left to struggle with the difficulties of a barbarous dialect whilst he preached the gospel to the natives of Gaul. The divine inspiration, whether it was conveyed in the form of a waking or of a sleeping vision, is described as a favour very liberally bestowed on all ranks of the faithful, on women as on elders, on boys as well as upon bishops. When their devout minds were sufficiently prepared by a course of prayer, of fasting, and of vigils, to receive the extraordinary impulse, they were transported out of their senses, and delivered in extasy what was inspired, being mere organs of the Holy Spirit, just as a pipe or flute is of him who blows into it. We may add that the design of these visions was, for the most part, either to disclose the future history, or to guide the present administration, of the church. The expulsion of the dæmons from the bodies of those unhappy persons whom they had been permitted to torment was considered as a signal, though ordinary, triumph of religion, and is repeatedly alleged by the ancient apologists as the most convincing evidence of the truth of Christianity. The awful ceremony was usually performed in a public manner, and in the presence of a great number of spectators; the patient was relieved by the power or skill of the exorcist, and the vanquished dæmon was heard to confess that he was one of the fabled gods of antiquity, who had impiously usurped the adoration of mankind. But the miraculous cure of diseases, of the most inveterate or even præternatural kind, can no longer occasion any surprise, when we recollect that in the days of Irenæus, about the end of the second century, the resurrection of the dead was very far from being esteemed an uncommon event; that the miracle was frequently performed on necessary occasions, by great fasting and the joint supplication of the church of the place, and that the persons thus restored to their prayers had lived afterwards among them many years. At such a period, when faith could boast of so many wonderful victories over death, it seems difficult to account for the scepticism of those philosophers who still rejected and derided the doctrine of the resurrection. A noble Grecian had rested on this important ground the whole controversy, and promised Theophilus, bishop of Antioch, that if he could be gratified with the sight of a single person who had been actually raised from the dead, he would immediately embrace the Christian religion. It is somewhat remarkable that the prelate of the first eastern church, however anxious for the conversion of his friend, thought proper to decline this fair and reasonable challenge.

The miracles of the primitive church, after obtaining the sanction of ages, have been lately attacked in a very free and ingenious inquiry; [1] which, though it has met with the most favourable reception from the Public, appears to have excited a general scandal among the divines of our own as well as of the other

[1] Dr. Middleton sent out his Introduction in the year 1747, published his Free Inquiry in 1749, and before his death, which happened in 1750, he had prepared a vindication of it against his numerous adversaries.

Protestant churches of Europe.[1] Our different sentiments on this subject will be much less influenced by
any particular arguments than by our habits of study
and reflection; and, above all, by the degree of the
evidence which we have accustomed ourselves to
require for the proof of a miraculous event. The
duty of an historian does not call upon him to inter-
pose his private judgment in this nice and important
controversy; but he ought not to dissemble the
difficulty of adopting such a theory as may reconcile
the interest of religion with that of reason, of making
a proper application of that theory, and of defining
with precision the limits of that happy period,
exempt from error and from deceit, to which we might
be disposed to extend the gift of supernatural powers.
From the first of the fathers to the last of the popes,
a succession of bishops, of saints, of martyrs, and of
miracles is continued without interruption, and the
progress of superstition was so gradual and almost
imperceptible that we know not in what particular
link we should break the chain of tradition. Every
age bears testimony to the wonderful events by which
it was distinguished, and its testimony appears no
less weighty and respectable than that of the preceding
generation, till we are insensibly led on to accuse our
own inconsistency, if in the eighth or in the twelfth
century we deny to the venerable Bede, or to the holy
Bernard, the same degree of confidence which in the
second century we had so liberally granted to Justin
or to Irenæus. If the truth of any of those miracles
is appreciated by their apparent use and propriety,
every age had unbelievers to convince, heretics to
confute, and idolatrous nations to convert; and
sufficient motives might always be produced to justify
the interposition of Heaven. And yet, since every
friend to revelation is persuaded of the reality, and
every reasonable man is convinced of the cessation,
of miraculous powers, it is evident that there must

[1] The university of Oxford conferred degrees on his
opponents. From the indignation of Mosheim we may
discover the sentiments of Lutheran divines.

have been *some period* in which they were either suddenly or gradually withdrawn from the Christian church. Whatever æra is chosen for that purpose, the death of the apostles, the conversion of the Roman empire, or the extinction of the Arian heresy, the insensibility of the Christians who lived at that time will equally afford a just matter of surprise. They still supported their pretensions after they had lost their power. Credulity performed the office of faith; fanaticism was permitted to assume the language of inspiration, and the effects of accident or contrivance were ascribed to supernatural causes. The recent experience of genuine miracles should have instructed the Christian world in the ways of Providence, and habituated their eye (if we may use a very inadequate expression) to the style of the divine artist. Should the most skilful painter of modern Italy presume to decorate his feeble imitations with the name of Raphael or of Correggio, the insolent fraud would be soon discovered and indignantly rejected.

Whatever opinion may be entertained of the miracles of the primitive church since the time of the apostles, this unresisting softness of temper, so conspicuous among the believers of the second and third centuries, proved of some accidental benefit to the cause of truth and religion. In modern times, a latent, and even involuntary, scepticism adheres to the most pious dispositions. Their admission of supernatural truths is much less an active consent than a cold and passive acquiescence. Accustomed long since to observe and to respect the invariable order of Nature, our reason, or at least our imagination, is not sufficiently prepared to sustain the visible action of the Deity. But in the first ages of Christianity the situation of mankind was extremely different. The most curious, or the most credulous, among the Pagans were often persuaded to enter into a society which asserted an actual claim of miraculous powers. The primitive Christians perpetually trod on mystic ground, and their minds were exercised by the habits of believing the most extraordinary events. They felt, or they fancied, that on every side they were incessantly assaulted by dæmons, comforted by visions, instructed by prophecy, and surprisingly delivered from danger, sickness, and from death itself, by the supplications of the church. The real or imaginary prodigies of which they so frequently conceived themselves to be the objects, the instruments, or the spectators, very happily disposed them to adopt, with the same ease, but with far greater justice, the authentic wonders of the evangelic history; and thus miracles that exceeded not the measure of their own experience inspired them with the most lively assurance of mysteries which were acknowledged to surpass the limits of their understanding. It is this deep impression of supernatural truths which has been so much celebrated under the name of faith; a state of mind described as the surest pledge of the divine favour and of future felicity, and recommended as the first or perhaps the only merit of a Christian. According to the more rigid doctors, the moral virtues, which may be equally practised by infidels, are destitute of any value or efficacy in the work of our justification.

IV. But the primitive Christian demonstrated his faith by his virtues; and it was very justly supposed that the divine persuasion, which enlightened or subdued the understanding, must, at the same time, purify the heart, and direct the actions, of the believer. The first apologists of Christianity who justify the innocence of their brethren, and the writers of a later period who celebrate the sanctity of their ancestors. display in the most lively colours the reformation of manners which was introduced into the world by the preaching of the gospel. As it is my intention to remark only such human causes as were permitted to second the influence of revelation, I shall slightly mention two motives which might naturally render the lives of the primitive Christians much purer and more austere than those of their Pagan contemporaries, or their degenerate successors; repentance for their past sins, and the laudable desire of supporting the reputation of the society in which they were engaged.

It is a very ancient reproach, suggested by the ignorance or the malice of infidelity, that the Christians allured into their party the most atrocious criminals, who, as soon as they were touched by a sense of remorse, were easily persuaded to wash away, in the water of baptism, the guilt of their past conduct, for which the temples of the gods refused to grant them any expiation. But this reproach, when it is cleared from misrepresentation, contributes as much to the honour as it did to the increase of the church. The friends of Christianity may acknowledge without a blush that many of the most eminent saints had been before their baptism the most abandoned sinners. Those persons who in the world had followed, though in an imperfect manner, the dictates of benevolence and propriety, derived such a calm satisfaction from the opinion of their own rectitude, as rendered them much less susceptible of the sudden emotions of shame, of grief, and of terror, which have given birth to so many wonderful conversions. After the example of their Divine Master, the missionaries of the gospel disdained not the society of men, and especially of women, oppressed by the consciousness, and very often by the effects, of their vices. As they emerged from sin and superstition to the glorious hope of immortality, they resolved to devote themselves to a life, not only of virtue, but of penitence. The desire of perfection became the ruling passion of their soul; and it is well known that, while reason embraces a cold mediocrity, our passions hurry us, with rapid violence, over the space which lies between the most opposite extremes.

When the new converts had been enrolled in the number of the faithful and were admitted to the sacraments of the church, they found themselves restrained from relapsing into their past disorders by another consideration of a less spiritual, but of a very innocent and respectable, nature. Any particular society that has departed from the great body of the nation or the religion to which it belonged immediately becomes the object of universal as well as invidious observation. In proportion to the smallness of its numbers, the character of the society may be affected by the virtue and vices of the persons who compose it; and every member is engaged to watch with the most vigilant attention over his own behaviour and over that of his brethren, since, as he must expect to incur a part of the common disgrace, he may hope to enjoy a share of the common reputation. When the Christians of Bithynia were brought before the tribunal of the younger Pliny, they assured the proconsul that, far from being engaged in any unlawful conspiracy, they were bound by a solemn obligation to abstain from the commission of those crimes which disturb the private or public peace of society, from theft, robbery, adultery, perjury, and fraud. Near a century afterwards, Tertullian, with an honest pride, could boast that very few Christians had suffered by the hand of the executioner, except on account of their religion. Their serious and sequestered life, averse to the gay luxury of the age, insured them to chastity, temperance, economy, and all the sober and domestic virtues. As the greater number were of some trade or profession, it was incumbent on them, by the strictest integrity and the fairest dealing, to remove the suspicions which the profane are too apt to conceive against the appearances of sanctity. The contempt of the world exercised them in the habits of humility, meekness, and patience. The more they were persecuted, the more closely they adhered to each other. Their mutual charity and unsuspecting confidence has been remarked by infidels, and was too often abused by perfidious friends.

It is a very honourable circumstance for the morals of the primitive Christians, that even their faults, or rather errors, were derived from an excess of virtue. The bishops and doctors of the church, whose evidence attests, and whose authority might influence, the professions, the principles, and even the practice, of their contemporaries, had studied the scriptures with less skill than devotion, and they often received, in the most literal sense, those rigid precepts of Christ and the apostles to which the prudence of succeeding commentators has applied a looser and more figurative mode of interpretation. Ambitious to exalt the perfection of the gospel above the wisdom of philosophy, the zealous fathers have carried the duties of self-mortification, of purity, and of patience, to a height which it is scarcely possible to attain, and much less to preserve, in our present state of weakness and corruption. A doctrine so extraordinary and so sublime must inevitably command the veneration of the people; but it was ill calculated to obtain the suffrage of those worldly philosophers who, in the conduct of this transitory life, consult only the feelings of nature and the interest of society.

There are two very natural propensities which we may distinguish in the most virtuous and liberal dispositions, the love of pleasure and the love of action. If the former be refined by art and learning, improved by the charms of social intercourse, and corrected by a just regard to economy, to health, and to reputation, it is productive of the greatest part of the happiness of private life. The love of action is a principle of a much stronger and more doubtful nature. It often leads to anger, to ambition, and to revenge; but, when it is guided by the sense of propriety and benevolence, it becomes the parent of every virtue; and if those virtues are accompanied with equal abilities, a family, a state, or an empire may be indebted for their safety and prosperity to the undaunted courage of a single man. To the love of pleasure we may therefore ascribe most of the agreeable, to the love of action we may attribute most of the useful and respectable, qualifications. The character in which both the one and the other should be united and harmonized would seem to constitute the most perfect idea of human nature. The insensible and inactive disposition, which should be supposed alike destitute of both, would be rejected, by the common consent of mankind, as utterly incapable of procuring any happiness to the individual, or any public benefit to the world. But it was not in *this* world that the primitive Christians were desirous of making themselves either agreeable or useful.

The acquisition of knowledge, the exercise of our reason or fancy, and the cheerful flow of unguarded conversation, may employ the leisure of a liberal mind. Such amusements, however, were rejected with abhorrence, or admitted with the utmost caution, by the severity of the fathers, who despised all knowledge that was not useful to salvation, and who considered all levity of discourse as a criminal abuse of the gift of speech. In our present state of existence, the body is so inseparably connected with the soul that it seems to be our interest to taste, with innocence and moderation, the enjoyments of which that faithful companion is susceptible. Very different was the reasoning of our devout predecessors; vainly aspiring to imitate the perfection of angels, they disdained, or they affected to disdain, every earthly and corporeal delight. Some of our senses indeed are necessary for our preservation, others for our subsistence, and others again for our information, and thus far it was impossible to reject the use of them. The first sensation of pleasure was marked as the first moment of their abuse. The unfeeling candidate for Heaven was instructed, not only to resist the grosser allurements of the taste or smell, but even to shut his ears against the profane harmony of sounds, and to view with indifference the most finished productions of human art. Gay apparel, magnificent houses, and elegant furniture were supposed to unite the double guilt of pride and of sensuality : a simple and mortified appearance was more suitable to the Christian who was certain of his sins and doubtful of his salvation. In their censures of luxury, the fathers are extremely minute and circumstantial; and among the various articles which excite their pious indignation, we may enumerate false hair, garments of any colour except white, instruments of music, vases of gold or silver, downy pillows (as Jacob reposed his head on a stone), white bread, foreign wines, public salutations, the use of warm baths, and the practice of shaving the beard, which, according to the expression of Tertullian, is a lie against our own faces, and an impious attempt to

improve the works of the Creator.   When Christianity
was introduced among the rich and the polite, the
observation of these singular laws was left, as it would
be at present, to the few who were ambitious of
superior sanctity.   But it is always easy, as well as
agreeable, for the inferior ranks of mankind to claim
a merit from the contempt of that pomp and pleasure
which fortune has placed beyond their reach.   The
virtue of the primitive Christians, like that of the first
Romans, was very frequently guarded by poverty and
ignorance.

The chaste severity of the fathers, in whatever
related to the commerce of the two sexes, flowed from
the same principle : their abhorrence of every enjoyment which might gratify the sensual and degrade
the spiritual nature of man.   It was their favourite
opinion that, if Adam had preserved his obedience to
the Creator, he would have lived for ever in a state of
virgin purity, and that some harmless mode of
vegetation might have peopled paradise with a race
of innocent and immortal beings.   The use of marriage
was permitted only to his fallen posterity, as a
necessary expedient to continue the human species,
and as a restraint, however imperfect, on the natural
licentiousness of desire.   The hesitation of the
orthodox casuists on this interesting subject betrays
the perplexity of men unwilling to approve an
institution which they were compelled to tolerate.
The enumeration of the very whimsical laws which
they most circumstantially imposed on the marriage-
bed, would force a smile from the young, and a blush
from the fair.   It was their unanimous sentiment that
a first marriage was adequate to all the purposes of
nature and of society.   The sensual connexion was
refined into a resemblance of the mystic union of
Christ with his church, and was pronounced to be
indissoluble either by divorce or by death.   The
practice of second nuptials was branded with the
name of a legal adultery ; and the persons who were
guilty of so scandalous an offence against Christian
purity were soon excluded from the honours, and even

from the alms, of the church. Since desire was imputed as a crime, and marriage was tolerated as a defect, it was consistent with the same principles to consider a state of celibacy as the nearest approach to the divine perfection. It was with the utmost difficulty that ancient Rome could support the institution of six vestals; but the primitive church was filled with a great number of persons of either sex who had devoted themselves to the profession of perpetual chastity. A few of these, among whom we may reckon the learned Origen, judged it the most prudent to disarm the tempter. Some were insensible and some were invincible against the assaults of the flesh. Disdaining an ignominious flight, the virgins of the warm climate of Africa encountered the enemy in the closest engagement; they permitted priests and deacons to share their bed, and gloried amidst the flames in their unsullied purity. But insulted Nature sometimes vindicated her rights, and this new species of martyrdom served only to introduce a new scandal into the church. Among the Christian ascetics, however (a name which they soon acquired from their painful exercise), many, as they were less presumptuous, were probably more successful. The loss of sensual pleasure was supplied and compensated by spiritual pride. Even the multitude of Pagans were inclined to estimate the merit of the sacrifice by its apparent difficulty; and it was in the praise of these chaste spouses of Christ that the fathers have poured forth the troubled stream of their eloquence. Such are the early traces of monastic principles and institutions which, in a subsequent age, have counterbalanced all the temporal advantages of Christianity.

The Christians were not less averse to the business than to the pleasures of this world. The defence of our persons and property they knew not how to reconcile with the patient doctrine which enjoined an unlimited forgiveness of past injuries and commanded them to invite the repetition of fresh insults. Their simplicity was offended by the use of oaths, by the pomp of magistracy, and by the active contention of public life, nor could their humane ignorance be convinced that it was lawful on any occasion to shed the blood of our fellow-creatures, either by the sword of justice or by that of war; even though their criminal or hostile attempts should threaten the peace and safety of the whole community. It was acknowledged that, under a less perfect law, the powers of the Jewish constitution had been exercised, with the approbation of Heaven, by inspired prophets and by anointed kings. The Christians felt and confessed that such institutions might be necessary for the present system of the world, and they cheerfully submitted to the authority of their Pagan governors. But, while they inculcated the maxims of passive obedience, they refused to take any active part in the civil administration or the military defence of the empire. Some indulgence might perhaps be allowed to those persons who, before their conversion, were already engaged in such violent and sanguinary occupations; but it was impossible that the Christians, without renouncing a more sacred duty, could assume the character of soldiers, of magistrates, or of princes. This indolent, or even criminal, disregard to the public welfare exposed them to the contempt and reproaches of the Pagans, who very frequently asked, What must be the fate of the empire, attacked on every side by the barbarians, if all mankind should adopt the pusillanimous sentiments of the new sect? To this insulting question the Christian apologists returned obscure and ambiguous answers, as they were unwilling to reveal the secret cause of their security; the expectation that, before the conversion of mankind was accomplished, war, government, the Roman empire and the world itself would be no more. It may be observed that, in this instance likewise, the situation of the first Christians coincided very happily with their religious scruples, and that their aversion to an active life contributed rather to excuse them from the service than to exclude them from the honours of the state and army.

V. But the human character, however it may be

exalted or depressed by a temporary enthusiasm, will return, by degrees, to its proper and natural level, and will resume those passions that seem the most adapted to its present condition. The primitive Christians were dead to the business and pleasures of the world; but their love of action, which could never be entirely extinguished, soon revived, and found a new occupation in the government of the church. A separate society, which attacked the established religion of the empire, was obliged to adopt some form of internal policy, and to appoint a sufficient number of ministers, intrusted not only with the spiritual functions, but even with the temporal direction, of the Christian commonwealth. The safety of that society, its honour, its aggrandisement, were productive, even in the most pious minds, of a spirit of patriotism such as the first of the Romans had felt for the republic, and sometimes, of a similar indifference in the use of whatever means might probably conduce to so desirable an end. The ambition of raising themselves or their friends to the honours and offices of the church was disguised by the laudable intention of devoting to the public benefit the power and consideration which, for that purpose only, it became their duty to solicit. In the exercise of their functions, they were frequently called upon to detect the errors of heresy, or the arts of faction, to oppose the designs of perfidious brethren, to stigmatize their characters with deserved infamy, and to expel them from the bosom of a society whose peace and happiness they had attempted to disturb. The ecclesiastical governors of the Christians were taught to unite the wisdom of the serpent with the innocence of the dove; but, as the former was refined, so the latter was insensibly corrupted, by the habits of government. In the church as well as in the world the persons who were placed in any public station rendered themselves considerable by their eloquence and firmness, by their knowledge of mankind, and by their dexterity in business; and, while they concealed from others, and, perhaps, from themselves, the secret motives of their conduct, they too frequently relapsed into all the turbulent passions of active life, which were tinctured with an additional degree of bitterness and obstinacy from the infusion of spiritual zeal.

The government of the church has often been the subject, as well as the prize, of religious contention. The hostile disputants of Rome, of Paris, of Oxford and of Geneva have alike struggled to reduce the primitive and apostolic model to the respective standards of their own policy. The few who have pursued this inquiry with more candour and impartiality are of opinion that the apostles declined the office of legislation, and rather chose to endure some partial scandals and divisions than to exclude the Christians of a future age from the liberty of varying their forms of ecclesiastical government according to the changes of times and circumstances. The scheme of policy which, under their approbation, was adopted for the use of the first century may be discovered from the practice of Jerusalem, of Ephesus, or of Corinth. The societies which were instituted in the cities of the Roman empire were united only by the ties of faith and charity. Independence and equality formed the basis of their internal constitution. The want of discipline and human learning was supplied by the occasional assistance of the *prophets*, who were called to that function, without distinction of age, of sex, or of natural abilities, and who, as often as they felt the divine impulse, poured forth the effusions of the spirit in the assembly of the faithful. But these extraordinary gifts were frequently abused or misapplied by the prophetic teachers. They displayed them at an improper season, presumptuously disturbed the service of the assembly, and by their pride or mistaken zeal they introduced, particularly into the apostolic church of Corinth, a long and melancholy train of disorders. As the institution of prophets became useless, and even pernicious, their powers were withdrawn and their office abolished. The public functions of religion were solely intrusted to the established ministers of the church, the *bishops* and the *presbyters ;* two appellations which, in their first origin, appear to have distinguished the same office and the same order of persons. The name of Presbyter was expressive of their age, or rather of their gravity and wisdom. The title of Bishop denoted their inspection over the faith and manners of the Christians who were committed to their pastoral care. In proportion to the respective numbers of the faithful, a larger or smaller number of these *episcopal presbyters* guided each infant congregation with equal authority and with united councils.

But the most perfect equality of freedom requires the directing hand of a superior magistrate; and the order of public deliberations soon introduces the office of a president, invested at least with the authority of collecting the sentiments, and of executing the resolutions, of the assembly. A regard for the public tranquillity, which would so frequently have been interrupted by annual or by occasional elections, induced the primitive Christians to constitute an honourable and perpetual magistracy, and to choose one of the wisest and most holy among their presbyters to execute, during his life, the duties of their ecclesiastical governor. It was under these circumstances that the lofty title of Bishop began to raise itself above the humble appellation of presbyter; and, while the latter remained the most natural distinction for the members of every Christian senate, the former was appropriated to the dignity of its new president. The advantages of this episcopal form of government, which appears to have been introduced before the end of the first century, were so obvious, and so important for the future greatness, as well as the present peace, of Christianity, that it was adopted without delay by all the societies which were already scattered over the empire, had acquired in a very early period the sanction of antiquity, and is still revered by the most powerful churches, both of the East and of the West, as a primitive and even as a divine establishment. It is needless to observe that the

pious and humble presbyters who were first dignified
with the episcopal title could not possess, and would
probably have rejected, the power and pomp which
now encircles the tiara of the Roman pontiff, or the
mitre of a German prelate. But we may define in
a few words the narrow limits of their original jurisdiction, which was chiefly of a spiritual, though in
some instances of a temporal, nature. It consisted
in the administration of the sacraments and discipline
of the church, the superintendency of religious ceremonies, which imperceptibly increased in number and
variety, the consecration of ecclesiastical ministers,
to whom the bishop assigned their respective functions,
the management of the public fund, and the determination of all such differences as the faithful were
unwilling to expose before the tribunal of an idolatrous
judge. These powers, during a short period, were
exercised according to the advice of the presbyteral
college, and with the consent and approbation of the
assembly of Christians. The primitive bishops were
considered only as the first of their equals, and the
honourable servants of a free people. Whenever
the episcopal chair became vacant by death, a new
president was chosen among the presbyters by the
suffrage of the whole congregation, every member of
which supposed himself invested with a sacred and
sacerdotal character.

Such was the mild and equal constitution by which
the Christians were governed more than a hundred
years after the death of the apostles. Every society
formed within itself a separate and independent
republic : and, although the most distant of these
little states maintained a mutual as well as friendly
intercourse of letters and deputations, the Christian
world was not yet connected by any supreme authority
or legislative assembly. As the numbers of the faithful were gradually multiplied, they discovered the
advantages that might result from a closer union of
their interest and designs. Towards the end of the
second century, the churches of Greece and Asia
adopted the useful institutions of provincial synods,

and they may justly be supposed to have borrowed the model of a representative council from the celebrated examples of their own country, the Amphictyons, the Achæan league, or the assemblies of the Ionian cities. It was soon established as a custom and as a law that the bishops of the independent churches should meet in the capital of the province at the stated periods of spring and autumn. Their deliberations were assisted by the advice of a few distinguished presbyters, and moderated by the presence of a listening multitude. Their decrees, which were styled Canons, regulated every important controversy of faith and discipline; and it was natural to believe that a liberal effusion of the Holy Spirit would be poured on the united assembly of the delegates of the Christian people. The institution of synods was so well suited to private ambition and to public interest that in the space of a few years it was received throughout the whole empire. A regular correspondence was established between the provincial councils, which mutually communicated and approved their respective proceedings; and the Catholic church soon assumed the form, and acquired the strength, of a great federative republic.

As the legislative authority of the particular churches was insensibly superseded by the use of councils, the bishops obtained by their alliance a much larger share of executive and arbitrary power; and, as soon as they were connected by a sense of their common interest, they were enabled to attack with united vigour the original rights of their clergy and people. The prelates of the third century imperceptibly changed the language of exhortation into that of command, scattered the seeds of future usurpations, and supplied, by scripture allegories and declamatory rhetoric, their deficiency of force and of reason. They exalted the unity and power of the church, as it was represented in the EPISCOPAL OFFICE, of which every bishop enjoyed an equal and undivided portion. Princes and magistrates, it was often repeated, might boast an earthly claim to a transitory dominion; it

was the episcopal authority alone which was derived
from the Deity, and extended itself over this and over
another world. The bishops were the vicegerents of
Christ, the successors of the apostles, and the mystic
substitutes of the high priest of the Mosaic law.
Their exclusive privilege of conferring the sacerdotal
character invaded the freedom both of clerical and of
popular elections; and if, in the administration of
the church, they still consulted the judgment of the
presbyters or the inclination of the people, they most
carefully inculcated the merit of such a voluntary
condescension. The bishops acknowledged the supreme authority which resided in the assembly of
their brethren; but, in the government of his peculiar
diocese, each of them exacted from his *flock* the same
implicit obedience as if that favourite metaphor had
been literally just, and as if the shepherd had been
of a more exalted nature than that of his sheep. This
obedience, however, was not imposed without some
efforts on one side and some resistance on the other.
The democratical part of the constitution was, in
many places, very warmly supported by the zealous
or interested opposition of the inferior clergy. But
their patriotism received the ignominious epithets of
faction and schism; and the episcopal cause was
indebted for its rapid progress to the labours of many
active prelates, who, like Cyprian of Carthage, could
reconcile the arts of the most ambitious statesman
with the Christian virtues which seem adapted to the
character of a saint and martyr.

The same causes which at first had destroyed the
equality of the presbyters introduced among the
bishops a pre-eminence of rank, and from thence a
superiority of jurisdiction. As often as in the spring
and autumn they met in provincial synod, the difference of personal merit and reputation was very
sensibly felt among the members of the assembly, and
the multitude was governed by the wisdom and
eloquence of the few. But the order of public proceedings required a more regular and less invidious
distinction; the office of perpetual presidents in the

councils of each province was conferred on the bishops
of the principal city, and these aspiring prelates, who
soon acquired the lofty titles of Metropolitans and
Primates, secretly prepared themselves to usurp over
their episcopal brethren the same authority which the
bishops had so lately assumed above the college of
presbyters. Nor was it long before an emulation
of pre-eminence and power prevailed among the
metropolitans themselves, each of them affecting to
display, in the most pompous terms, the temporal
honours and advantages of the city over which he
presided; the numbers and opulence of the Christians
who were subject to their pastoral care; the saints
and martyrs who had arisen among them, and the
purity with which they preserved the tradition of the
faith, as it had been transmitted through a series of
orthodox bishops from the apostle or the apostolic
disciple to whom the foundation of their church was
ascribed. From every cause, either of a civil or of an
ecclesiastical nature, it was easy to foresee that Rome
must enjoy the respect, and would soon claim the
obedience, of the provinces. The society of the faithful bore a just proportion to the capital of the empire;
and the Roman church was the greatest, the most
numerous, and, in regard to the West, the most
ancient of all the Christian establishments, many of
which had received their religion from the pious
labours of her missionaries. Instead of *one* apostolic
founder, the utmost boast of Antioch, of Ephesus, or
of Corinth, the banks of the Tiber were supposed to
have been honoured with the preaching and martyrdom of the *two* most eminent among the apostles;
and the bishops of Rome very prudently claimed the
inheritance of whatsoever prerogatives were attributed
either to the person or to the office of St. Peter. The
bishops of Italy and of the provinces were disposed to
allow them a primacy of order and association (such
was their very accurate expression) in the Christian
aristocracy. But the power of a monarch was rejected
with abhorrence, and the aspiring genius of Rome
experienced, from the nations of Asia and Africa, a

more vigorous resistance to her spiritual than she had formerly done to her temporal, dominion. The patriotic Cyprian, who ruled with the most absolute sway the church of Carthage and the provincial synods, opposed with resolution and success the ambition of the Roman pontiff, artfully connected his own cause with that of the eastern bishops, and, like Hannibal, sought out new allies in the heart of Asia. If this Punic war was carried on without any effusion of blood, it was owing much less to the moderation than to the weakness of the contending prelates. Invectives and excommunications were *their* only weapons; and these, during the progress of the whole controversy, they hurled against each other with equal fury and devotion. The hard necessity of censuring either a pope or a saint and martyr distresses the modern Catholics, whenever they are obliged to relate the particulars of a dispute in which the champions of religion indulged such passions as seem much more adapted to the senate or to the camp.

The progress of the ecclesiastical authority gave birth to the memorable distinction of the laity and of the clergy, which had been unknown to the Greeks and Romans. The former of these appellations comprehended the body of the Christian people; the latter, according to the signification of the word, was appropriated to the chosen portion that had been set apart for the service of religion; a celebrated order of men which has furnished the most important, though not always the most edifying, subjects for modern history. Their mutual hostilities sometimes disturbed the peace of the infant church, but their zeal and activity were united in the common cause, and the love of power, which (under the most artful disguises) could insinuate itself into the breasts of bishops and martyrs, animated them to increase the number of their subjects and to enlarge the limits of the Christian empire. They were destitute of any temporal force, and they were for a long time discouraged and oppressed, rather than assisted, by the civil magistrate; but they had acquired, and they

employed within their own society, the two most
efficacious instruments of government, rewards and
punishments; the former derived from the pious
liberality, the latter from the devout apprehensions of
the faithful.

I. The community of goods, which had so agreeably
amused the imagination of Plato, and which subsisted
in some degree among the austere sect of the Essenians,
was adopted for a short time in the primitive church.
The fervour of the first proselytes prompted them to
sell those worldly possessions which they despised,
to lay the price of them at the feet of the apostles,
and to content themselves with receiving an equal
share out of the general distribution.   The progress
of the Christian religion relaxed, and gradually
abolished, this generous institution, which, in hands
less pure than those of the apostles, would too soon
have been corrupted and abused by the returning
selfishness of human nature; and the converts who
embraced the new religion were permitted to retain
the possession of their patrimony, to receive legacies
and inheritances, and to increase their separate
property by all the lawful means of trade and industry.
Instead of an absolute sacrifice, a moderate proportion
was accepted by the ministers of the gospel; and in
their weekly or monthly assemblies every believer,
according to the exigency of the occasion, and the
measure of his wealth and piety, presented his
voluntary offering for the use of the common fund.
Nothing, however inconsiderable, was refused; but
it was diligently inculcated that, in the article of
Tythes, the Mosaic law was still of divine obligation;
and that, since the Jews, under a less perfect discipline,
had been commanded to pay a tenth part of all that
they possessed, it would become the disciples of
Christ to distinguish themselves by a superior degree
of liberality, and to acquire some merit by resigning
a superfluous treasure, which must so soon be annihilated with the world itself.   It is almost unnecessary
to observe that the revenue of each particular church,
which was of so uncertain and fluctuating a nature,

must have varied with the poverty or the opulence of the faithful, as they were dispersed in obscure villages or collected in the great cities of the empire. In the time of the emperor Decius, it was the opinion of the magistrates that the Christians of Rome were possessed of very considerable wealth; that vessels of gold and silver were used in their religious worship; and that many among their proselytes had sold their lands and houses to increase the public riches of the sect, at the expense, indeed, of their unfortunate children, who found themselves beggars, because their parents had been saints. We should listen with distrust to the suspicions of strangers and enemies: on this occasion, however, they receive a very specious and probable colour from the two following circumstances, the only ones that have reached our knowledge which define any precise sums or convey any distinct idea. Almost at the same period, the bishop of Carthage, from a society less opulent than that of Rome, collected a hundred thousand sesterces (above eight hundred and fifty pounds sterling), on a sudden call of charity, to redeem the brethren of Numidia, who had been carried away captives by the barbarians of the desert. About an hundred years before the reign of Decius, the Roman church had received, in a single donation, the sum of two hundred thousand sesterces from a stranger of Pontus, who proposed to fix his residence in the capital. These oblations, for the most part, were made in money; nor was the society of Christians either desirous or capable of acquiring, to any considerable degree, the incumbrance of landed property. It had been provided by several laws, which were enacted with the same design as our statutes of mortmain, that no real estates should be given or bequeathed to any corporate body, without either a special privilege or a particular dispensation from the emperor or from the senate; who were seldom disposed to grant them in favour of a sect, at first the object of their contempt, and at last of their fears and jealousy. A transaction, however, is related under the reign of Alexander Severus, which discovers that the restraint was sometimes eluded or suspended, and that the Christians were permitted to claim and to possess lands within the limits of Rome itself. The progress of Christianity and the civil confusion of the empire contributed to relax the severity of the laws; and, before the close of the third century, many considerable estates were bestowed on the opulent churches of Rome, Milan, Carthage, Antioch, Alexandria, and the other great cities of Italy and the provinces.

The bishop was the natural steward of the church; the public stock was intrusted to his care, without account or control; the presbyters were confined to their spiritual functions, and the more dependent order of deacons was solely employed in the management and distribution of the ecclesiastical revenue. If we may give credit to the vehement declamations of Cyprian, there were too many among his African brethren who, in the execution of their charge, violated every precept, not only of evangelic perfection but even of moral virtue. By some of these unfaithful stewards, the riches of the church were lavished in sensual pleasures, by others they were perverted to the purposes of private gain, of fraudulent purchases, and of rapacious usury. But, as long as the contributions of the Christian people were free and unconstrained, the abuse of their confidence could not be very frequent, and the general uses to which their liberality was applied reflected honour on the religious society. A decent portion was reserved for the maintenance of the bishop and his clergy; a sufficient sum was allotted for the expenses of the public worship, of which the feasts of love, the *agapæ*, as they were called, constituted a very pleasing part. The whole remainder was the sacred patrimony of the poor. According to the discretion of the bishop, it was distributed to support widows and orphans, the lame, the sick, and the aged of the community; to comfort strangers and pilgrims, and to alleviate the misfortunes of prisoners and captives, more especially when their sufferings had been occasioned by their firm attachment to the cause of religion. A generous intercourse of charity united the most distant provinces, and the smaller congregations were cheerfully assisted by the alms of their more opulent brethren. Such an institution, which paid less regard to the merit than to the distress of the object, very materially conduced to the progress of Christianity. The Pagans who were actuated by a sense of humanity, while they derided the doctrines, acknowledged the benevolence, of the new sect. The prospect of immediate relief and of future protection allured into its hospitable bosom many of those unhappy persons whom the neglect of the world would have abandoned to the miseries of want, of sickness, and of old age. There is some reason likewise to believe that great numbers of infants who, according to the inhuman practice of the times, had been exposed by their parents were frequently rescued from death, baptized, educated, and maintained by the piety of the Christians, and at the expense of the public treasure.

II. It is the undoubted right of every society to exclude from its communion and benefits such among its members as reject or violate those regulations which have been established by general consent. In the exercise of this power, the censures of the Christian church were chiefly directed against scandalous sinners, and particularly those who were guilty of murder, of fraud, or of incontinence; against the authors, or the followers, of any heretical opinions which had been condemned by the judgment of the episcopal order; and against those unhappy persons who, whether from choice or from compulsion, had polluted themselves after their baptism by any act of idolatrous worship. The consequences of excommunication were of a temporal as well as a spiritual nature. The Christian against whom it was pronounced was deprived of any part in the oblations of the faithful. The ties both of religious and of private friendship were dissolved; he found himself a profane object of abhorrence to the persons whom he the most esteemed, or by whom he had been the most tenderly

beloved; and, as far as an expulsion from a respectable society could imprint on his character a mark of
disgrace, he was shunned or suspected by the gener-
ality of mankind.   The situation of these unfortunate
exiles was in itself very painful and melancholy; but,
as it usually happens, their apprehensions far exceeded
their sufferings.   The benefits of the Christian communion were those of eternal life, nor could they erase
from their minds the awful opinion that to those
ecclesiastical governors by whom they were condemned the Deity had committed the keys of Hell
and of Paradise.   The heretics, indeed, who might be
supported by the consciousness of their intentions,
and by the flattering hope that they alone had discovered the true path of salvation, endeavoured to
regain, in their separate assemblies, those comforts,
temporal as well as spiritual, which they no longer
derived from the great society of Christians.   But
almost all those who had reluctantly yielded to the
power of vice or idolatry were sensible of their fallen
condition, and anxiously desirous of being restored
to the benefits of the Christian communion.

With regard to the treatment of these penitents,
two opposite opinions, the one of justice, the other
of mercy, divided the primitive church.   The more
rigid and inflexible casuists refused them for ever,
and without exception, the meanest place in the holy
community, which they had disgraced or deserted,
and, leaving them to the remorse of a guilty conscience,
indulged them only with a faint ray of hope that the
contrition of their life and death might possibly be
accepted by the Supreme Being.   A milder sentiment
was embraced, in practice as well as in theory, by the
purest and most respectable of the Christian churches.
The gates of reconciliation and of Heaven were seldom
shut against the returning penitent;   but a severe
and solemn form of discipline was instituted, which,
while it served to expiate his crime, might powerfully
deter the spectators from the imitation of his example.
Humbled by a public confession, emaciated by fasting,
and clothed in sackcloth, the penitent lay prostrate

at the door of the assembly, imploring, with tears, the pardon of his offences, and soliciting the prayers of the faithful. If the fault was of a very heinous nature, whole years of penance were esteemed an inadequate satisfaction to the Divine Justice; and it was always by slow and painful gradations that the sinner, the heretic, or the apostate was re-admitted into the bosom of the church. A sentence of perpetual excommunication was, however, reserved for some crimes of an extraordinary magnitude, and particularly for the inexcusable relapses of those penitents who had already experienced and abused the clemency of their ecclesiastical superiors. According to the circumstances or the number of the guilty, the exercise of the Christian discipline was varied by the discretion of the bishops. The councils of Ancyra and Illiberis were held about the same time, the one in Galatia, the other in Spain; but their respective canons, which are still extant, seem to breathe a very different spirit. The Galatian, who after his baptism had repeatedly sacrificed to idols, might obtain his pardon by a penance of seven years, and, if he had seduced others to imitate his example, only three years more were added to the term of his exile. But the unhappy Spaniard who had committed the same offence was deprived of the hope of reconciliation, even in the article of death; and his idolatry was placed at the head of a list of seventeen other crimes, against which a sentence no less terrible was pronounced. Among these we may distinguish the inexpiable guilt of calumniating a bishop, a presbyter, or even a deacon.

The well-tempered mixture of liberality and rigour, the judicious dispensation of rewards and punishments, according to the maxims of policy as well as justice, constituted the *human* strength of the church. The bishops, whose paternal care extended itself to the government of both worlds, were sensible of the importance of these prerogatives, and, covering their ambition with the fair pretence of the love of order, they were jealous of any rival in the exercise of a discipline so necessary to prevent the desertion of those troops which had inlisted themselves under the banner of the cross, and whose numbers every day became more considerable. From the imperious declamations of Cyprian we should naturally conclude that the doctrines of excommunication and penance formed the most essential part of religion; and that it was much less dangerous for the disciples of Christ to neglect the observance of the moral duties than to despise the censures and authority of their bishops. Sometimes we might imagine that we were listening to the voice of Moses, when he commanded the earth to open, and to swallow up, in consuming flames, the rebellious race which refused obedience to the priesthood of Aaron; and we should sometimes suppose that we heard a Roman consul asserting the majesty of the republic, and declaring his inflexible resolution to enforce the rigour of the laws. " If such irregularities are suffered with impunity (it is thus that the bishop of Carthage chides the lenity of his colleague), if such irregularities are suffered, there is an end of EPISCOPAL VIGOUR; an end of the sublime and divine power of governing the church, an end of Christianity itself." Cyprian had renounced those temporal honours which it is probable he would never have obtained; but the acquisition of such absolute command over the consciences and understanding of a congregation, however obscure or despised by the world, is more truly grateful to the pride of the human heart than the possession of the most despotic power imposed by arms and conquest on a reluctant people.

In the course of this important, though perhaps tedious, inquiry I have attempted to display the secondary causes which so efficaciously assisted the truth of the Christian religion. If among these causes we have discovered any artificial ornaments, any accidental circumstances, or any mixture of error and passion, it cannot appear surprising that mankind should be the most sensibly affected by such motives as were suited to their imperfect nature. It was by the aid of these causes, exclusive zeal, the immediate expectation of another world, the claim of miracles, the practice of rigid virtue, and the constitution of the primitive church, that Christianity spread itself with so much success in the Roman empire. To the first of these the Christians were indebted for their invincible valour, which disdained to capitulate with the enemy whom they were resolved to vanquish. The three succeeding causes supplied their valour with the most formidable arms. The last of these causes united their courage, directed their arms, and gave their efforts that irresistible weight which even a small band of well-trained and intrepid volunteers has so often possessed over an undisciplined multitude, ignorant of the subject, and careless of the event of the war. In the various religions of Polytheism, some wandering fanatics of Egypt and Syria, who addressed themselves to the credulous superstition of the populace, were perhaps the only order of priests that derived their whole support and credit from their sacerdotal profession, and were very deeply affected by a personal concern for the safety or prosperity of their tutelar deities. The ministers of Polytheism, both in Rome and in the provinces, were for the most part men of a noble birth, and of an affluent fortune, who received, as an honourable distinction, the care of a celebrated temple, or of a public sacrifice, exhibited, very frequently at their own expense, the sacred games, and with cold indifference performed the ancient rites, according to the laws and fashion of their country. As they were engaged in the ordinary occupations of life, their zeal and devotion were seldom animated by a sense of interest, or by the habits of an ecclesiastical character. Confined to their respective temples and cities, they remained without any connexion of discipline or government; and, whilst they acknowledged the supreme jurisdiction of the senate, of the college of pontiffs, and of the emperor, those civil magistrates contented themselves with the easy task of maintaining in peace and dignity the general worship of mankind. We have already seen how various, how loose, and how uncertain were the religious sentiments of Polytheists. They were abandoned, almost without control, to the natural workings of a superstitious fancy. The accidental circumstances of their life and situation determined the object, as well as the degree, of their devotion; and, as long as their adoration was successively prostituted to a thousand deities, it was scarcely possible that their hearts could be susceptible of a very sincere or lively passion for any of them.

When Christianity appeared in the world, even these faint and imperfect impressions had lost much of their original power. Human reason, which, by its unassisted strength, is incapable of perceiving the mysteries of faith, had already obtained an easy triumph over the folly of Paganism; and, when Tertullian or Lactantius employ their labours in exposing its falsehood and extravagance, they are obliged to transcribe the eloquence of Cicero or the wit of Lucian. The contagion of these sceptical writings had been diffused far beyond the number of their readers. The fashion of incredulity was communicated from the philosopher to the man of pleasure or business, from the noble to the plebeian, and from the master to the menial slave who waited at his table, and who eagerly listened to the freedom of his conversation. On public occasions the philosophic part of mankind affected to treat with respect and decency the religious institutions of their country; but their secret contempt penetrated through the thin and awkward disguise; and even the people, when they discovered that their deities were rejected and derided by those whose rank or understanding they were accustomed to reverence, were filled with doubts and apprehensions concerning the truth of those doctrines to which they had yielded the most implicit belief. The decline of ancient prejudice exposed a very numerous portion of human kind to the danger of a painful and comfortless situation. A state of scepticism and suspense may amuse a few inquisitive minds. But the practice of superstition is so congenial to the multitude that, if they are forcibly awakened, they still regret the loss of their pleasing vision. Their love of the marvellous and super-natural, their curiosity with regard to future events, and their strong propensity to extend their hopes and fears beyond the limits of the visible world, were the principal causes which favoured the establishment of Polytheism. So urgent on the vulgar is the necessity of believing that the fall of any system of mythology will most probably be succeeded by the introduction of some other mode of superstition. Some deities of a more recent and fashionable cast might soon have occupied the deserted temples of Jupiter and Apollo, if, in the decisive moment, the wisdom of Providence had not interposed a genuine revelation, fitted to inspire the most rational esteem and conviction, whilst, at the same time, it was adorned with all that could attract the curiosity, the wonder, and the veneration of the people. In their actual disposition, as many were almost disengaged from their artificial prejudices, but equally susceptible and desirous of a devout attachment, an object much less deserving would have been sufficient to fill the vacant place in their hearts, and to gratify the uncertain eagerness of their passions. Those who are inclined to pursue this reflection, instead of viewing with astonishment the ragid progress of Christianity, will perhaps be sur-prised that its success was not still more rapid and still more universal.

It has been observed, with truth as well as pro-priety, that the conquests of Rome prepared and facilitated those of Christianity. In the second chapter of this work we have attempted to explain in what manner the most civilised provinces of Europe, Asia, and Africa were united under the dominion of one sovereign, and gradually connected by the most intimate ties of laws, of manners, and of language. The Jews of Palestine, who had fondly expected a temporal deliverer, gave so cold a reception to the miracles of the divine prophet that it was found unnecessary to publish, or at least to preserve, any Hebrew gospel. The authentic histories of the actions of Christ were composed in the Greek language, at a considerable distance from Jerusalem, and after the Gentile converts were grown extremely numerous. As soon as those histories were translated into the Latin tongue, they were perfectly intelligible to all the subjects of Rome, excepting only to the peasants of Syria and Egypt, for whose benefit particular versions were afterwards made. The public highways, which had been constructed for the use of the legions, opened an easy passage for the Christian missionaries from Damascus to Corinth, and from Italy to the extremity of Spain or Britain; nor did those spiritual conquerors encounter any of the obstacles which usually retard or prevent the introduction of a foreign religion into a distant country. There is the strongest reason to believe that before the reigns of Diocletian and Constantine the faith of Christ had been preached in every province, and in all the great cities of the empire; but the foundation of the several congregations, the numbers of the faithful who composed them, and their proportion to the unbelieving multitude, are now buried in obscurity, or disguised by fiction and declamation. Such imperfect circumstances, however, as have reached our knowledge concerning the increase of the Christian name in Asia and Greece, in Egypt, in Italy, and in the West, we shall now proceed to relate, without neglecting the real or imaginary acquisitions which lay beyond the frontiers of the Roman empire.

The rich provinces that extend from the Euphrates to the Ionian sea were the principal theatre on which the apostle of the Gentiles displayed his zeal and piety. The seeds of the gospel, which he had scattered in a fertile soil, were diligently cultivated by his disciples; and it should seem that, during the two first centuries, the most considerable body of Christians was contained within those limits. Among the societies which were instituted in Syria, none were more ancient or more illustrious than those of Damascus, of Berœa or Aleppo, and of Antioch. The prophetic introduction of the Apocalypse has described and immortalized the seven churches of Asia :—Ephesus, Smyrna, Pergamus, Thyatira, Sardes, Laodicea, and Philadelphia; and their colonies were soon diffused over that populous country. In a very early period, the islands of Cyprus and Crete, the provinces of Thrace and Macedonia, gave a favourable reception to the new religion; and Christian republics were soon founded in the cities of Corinth, of Sparta, and of Athens. The antiquity of the Greek and Asiatic churches allowed a sufficient space of time for their increase and multiplication, and even the swarms of Gnostics and other heretics serve to display the flourishing condition of the orthodox church, since the appellation of heretics has always been applied to the less numerous party. To these domestic testimonies we may add the confession, the complaints, and the apprehensions of the Gentiles themselves. From the writings of Lucian, a philosopher who had studied mankind, and who describes their manners in the most lively colours, we may learn that, under the reign of Commodus, his native country of Pontus was filled with Epicureans and *Christians*. Within fourscore years after the death of Christ, the humane Pliny laments the magnitude of the evil which he vainly attempted to eradicate. In his very curious epistle to the emperor Trajan, he affirms that the temples were almost deserted, that the sacred victims scarcely found any purchasers, and that the superstition had not only infected the cities, but had even spread itself into the villages and the open country of Pontus and Bithynia.

Without descending into a minute scrutiny of the expressions or of the motives of those writers who either celebrate or lament the progress of Christianity in the East, it may in general be observed that none of them have left us any grounds from whence a just estimate might be formed of the real numbers of the faithful in those provinces. One circumstance, however, has been fortunately preserved, which seems to cast a more distinct light on this obscure but interesting subject. Under the reign of Theodosius, after Christianity had enjoyed, during more than sixty years, the sunshine of Imperial favour, the ancient and illustrious church of Antioch consisted of one hundred thousand persons, three thousand of whom were supported out of the public oblations. The splendour and dignity of the queen of the East, the acknowledged populousness of Cæsarea, Seleucia, and Alexandria, and the destruction of two hundred and fifty thousand souls in the earthquake which afflicted Antioch under the elder Justin, are so many convincing proofs that the whole number of its inhabitants was not less than half a million, and that the Christians, however multiplied by zeal and power, did not exceed a fifth part of that great city. How different a proportion must we adopt when we compare the persecuted with the triumphant church, the West with the East, remote villages with populous towns, and countries recently converted to the faith with the place where the believers first received the appellation of Christians ! It must not, however, be dissembled that in another passage Chrysostom, to whom we are indebted for this useful information, computes the multitude of the faithful as even superior to that of the Jews and Pagans. But the solution of this apparent difficulty is easy and obvious. The eloquent preacher draws a parallel between the civil and the ecclesiastical constitution of Antioch; between the list of Christians who had acquired Heaven by baptism and the list of citizens who had a right to share the public liberality. Slaves, strangers, and infants were comprised in the former; they were excluded from the latter.

The extensive commerce of Alexandria, and its proximity to Palestine, gave an easy entrance to the new religion. It was at first embraced by great numbers of the Therapeutæ, or Essenians of the lake Mareotis, a Jewish sect which had abated much of its reverence for the Mosaic ceremonies. The austere life of the Essenians, their fasts and excommunications, the community of goods, the love of celibacy, their zeal for martyrdom, and the warmth though not the purity of their faith, already offered a very lively

image of the primitive discipline. It was in the school
of Alexandria that the Christian theology appears to
have assumed a regular and scientifical form; and,
when Hadrian visited Egypt, he found a church,
composed of Jews and of Greeks, sufficiently important to attract the notice of that inquisitive prince.
But the progress of Christianity was for a long time
confined within the limits of a single city, which was
itself a foreign colony, and, till the close of the second
century, the predecessors of Demetrius were the only
prelates of the Egyptian church. Three bishops were
consecrated by the hands of Demetrius, and the
number was increased to twenty by his successor
Heraclas. The body of the natives, a people distinguished by a sullen inflexibility of temper,
entertained the new doctrine with coldness and
reluctance; and even in the time of Origen it was rare
to meet with an Egyptian who had surmounted his
early prejudices in favour of the sacred animals of
his country. As soon, indeed, as Christianity
ascended the throne, the zeal of those barbarians
obeyed the prevailing impulsion; the cities of Egypt
were filled with bishops, and the deserts of Thebais
swarmed with hermits.

A perpetual stream of strangers and provincials
flowed into the capacious bosom of Rome. Whatever
was strange or odious, whoever was guilty or suspected, might hope, in the obscurity of that immense
capital, to elude the vigilance of the law. In such a
various conflux of nations, every teacher, either of
truth or of falsehood, every founder, whether of a
virtuous or a criminal association, might easily
multiply his disciples or accomplices. The Christians
of Rome, at the time of the accidental persecution of
Nero, are represented by Tacitus as already amounting
to a very great multitude, and the language of that
great historian is almost similar to the style employed
by Livy when he relates the introduction and the
suppression of the rites of Bacchus. After the Bac-
chanals had awakened the severity of the senate, it
was likewise apprehended that a very great multitude,

as it were *another people,* had been initiated into those abhorred mysteries. A more careful inquiry soon demonstrated that the offenders did not exceed seven thousand; a number, indeed, sufficiently alarming, when considered as the object of public justice. It is with the same candid allowance that we should interpret the vague expressions of Tacitus, and in a former instance of Pliny, when they exaggerate the crowds of deluded fanatics who had forsaken the established worship of the gods. The church of Rome was undoubtedly the first and most populous of the empire; and we are possessed of an authentic record which attests the state of religion in that city, about the middle of the third century, and after a peace of thirty-eight years. The clergy, at that time, consisted of a bishop, forty-six presbyters, seven deacons, as many sub-deacons, forty-two acolytes, and fifty readers, exorcists, and porters. The number of widows, of the infirm, and of the poor, who were maintained by the oblations of the faithful, amounted to fifteen hundred. From reason, as well as from the analogy of Antioch, we may venture to estimate the Christians of Rome at about fifty thousand. The populousness of that great capital cannot, perhaps, be exactly ascertained; but the most modest calculation will not surely reduce it lower than a million of inhabitants, of whom the Christians might constitute at the most a twentieth part.

The western provincials appeared to have derived the knowledge of Christianity from the same source which had diffused among them the language, the sentiments, and the manners of Rome. In this more important circumstance, Africa, as well as Gaul, was gradually fashioned to the imitation of the capital. Yet, notwithstanding the many favourable occasions which might invite the Roman missionaries to visit their Latin provinces, it was late before they passed either the sea or the Alps; nor can we discover in those great countries any assured traces either of faith or of persecution that ascend higher than the reign of the Antonines. The slow progress of the gospel in the cold climate of Gaul was extremely different from the eagerness with which it seems to have been received on the burning sands of Africa. The African Christians soon formed one of the principal members of the primitive church. The practice introduced into that province of appointing bishops to the most inconsiderable towns, and very frequently to the most obscure villages, contributed to multiply the splendour and importance of their religious societies, which during the course of the third century were animated by the zeal of Tertullian, directed by the abilities of Cyprian, and adorned by the eloquence of Lactantius. But if, on the contrary, we turn our eyes towards Gaul, we must content ourselves with discovering, in the time of Marcus Antoninus, the feeble and united congregations of Lyons and Vienna; and even as late as the reign of Decius we are assured that in a few cities only, Arles, Narbonne, Toulouse, Limoges, Clermont, Tours, and Paris, some scattered churches were supported by the devotion of a small number of Christians. Silence is indeed very consistent with devotion, but, as it is seldom compatible with zeal, we may perceive and lament the languid state of Christianity in those provinces which had exchanged the Celtic for the Latin tongue; since they did not, during the three first centuries, give birth to a single ecclesiastical writer. From Gaul, which claimed a just pre-eminence of learning and authority over all the countries on this side of the Alps, the light of the gospel was more faintly reflected on the remote provinces of Spain and Britain; and, if we may credit the vehement assertions of Tertullian, they had already received the first rays of the faith when he addressed his apology to the magistrates of the emperor Severus. But the obscure and imperfect origin of the western churches of Europe has been so negligently recorded that, if we would relate the time and manner of their foundation, we must supply the silence of antiquity by those legends which avarice or superstition long afterwards dictated to the monks in the lazy gloom of their convents. Of these holy romances, that of the apostle St. James can alone, by its single extravagance, deserve to be mentioned. From a peaceful fisherman of the lake of Gennesareth, he was transformed into a valorous knight, who charged at the head of the Spanish chivalry in their battles against the Moors. The gravest historians have celebrated his exploits; the miraculous shrine of Compostella displayed his power; and the sword of a military order, assisted by the terrors of the Inquisition, was sufficient to remove every objection of profane criticism.

The progress of Christianity was not confined to the Roman empire; and, according to the primitive fathers, who interpret facts by prophecy, the new religion within a century after the death of its divine author had already visited every part of the globe. "There exists not," says Justin Martyr, "a people, whether Greek or barbarian, or any other race of men, by whatsoever appellation or manners they may be distinguished, however ignorant of arts or agriculture, whether they dwell under tents, or wander about in covered waggons, among whom prayers are not offered up in the name of a crucified Jesus to the Father and Creator of all things." But this splendid exaggeration, which even at present it would be extremely difficult to reconcile with the real state of mankind, can be considered only as the rash sally of a devout but careless writer, the measure of whose belief was regulated by that of his wishes. But neither the belief nor the wishes of the fathers can alter the truth of history. It will still remain an undoubted fact that the barbarians of Scythia and Germany who afterwards subverted the Roman monarchy were involved in the darkness of paganism; and that even the conversion of Iberia, of Armenia, or of Æthiopia, was not attempted with any degree of success till the sceptre was in the hands of an orthodox emperor. Before that time the various accidents of war and commerce might indeed diffuse an imperfect knowledge of the gospel among the tribes of Caledonia, and among the borderers of the Rhine, the Danube, and the Euphrates. Beyond the last-mentioned river, Edessa was distinguished by a firm and early adherence to the faith. From Edessa the principles of Christianity were easily introduced into the Greek and Syrian cities which obeyed the successors of Artaxerxes; but they do not appear to have made any deep impression on the minds of the Persians, whose religious system, by the labours of a well-disciplined order of priests, had been constructed with much more art and solidity than the uncertain mythology of Greece and Rome.

From this impartial, though imperfect, survey of the progress of Christianity, it may perhaps seem probable that the number of its proselytes has been excessively magnified by fear on the one side and by devotion on the other. According to the irreproachable testimony of Origen, the proportion of the faithful was very inconsiderable when compared with the multitude of an unbelieving world; but, as we are left without any distinct information, it is impossible to determine, and it is difficult even to conjecture, the real numbers of the primitive Christians. The most favourable calculation, however, that can be deduced from the examples of Antioch and of Rome will not permit us to imagine that more than a twentieth part of the subjects of the empire had enlisted themselves under the banner of the cross before the important conversion of Constantine. But their habits of faith, of zeal, and of union seemed to multiply their numbers; and the same causes which contributed to their future increase served to render their actual strength more apparent and more formidable.

Such is the constitution of civil society that, whilst a few persons are distinguished by riches, by honours, and by knowledge, the body of the people is condemned to obscurity, ignorance, and poverty. The Christian religion, which addressed itself to the whole human race, must consequently collect a far greater number of proselytes from the lower than from the superior ranks of life. This innocent and natural circumstance has been improved into a very odious imputation, which seems to be less strenuously denied by the apologists than it is urged by the adversaries of the faith; that the new sect of Christians was almost entirely composed of the dregs of the populace, of peasants and mechanics, of boys and women, of beggars and slaves, the last of whom might sometimes introduce the missionaries into the rich and noble families to which they belonged. These obscure teachers (such was the charge of malice and infidelity) are as mute in public as they are loquacious and dogmatical in private. Whilst they cautiously avoid the dangerous encounter of philosophers, they mingle with the rude and illiterate crowd, and insinuate themselves into those minds whom their age, their sex, or their education has the best disposed to receive the impression of superstitious terrors.

This unfavourable picture, though not devoid of a faint resemblance, betrays, by its dark colouring and distorted features, the pencil of an enemy. As the humble faith of Christ diffused itself through the world, it was embraced by several persons who derived some consequence from the advantages of nature or fortune. Aristides, who presented an eloquent apology to the emperor Hadrian, was an Athenian philosopher. Justin Martyr had sought divine knowledge in the schools of Zeno, of Aristotle, of Pythagoras, and of Plato, before he fortunately was accosted by the old man, or rather the angel, who turned his attention to the study of the Jewish prophets. Clemens of Alexandria had acquired much various reading in the Greek, and Tertullian in the Latin language. Julius Africanus and Origen possessed a very considerable share of the learning of their times; and, although the style of Cyprian is very different from that of Lactantius, we might almost discover that both those writers had been public teachers of rhetoric. Even the study of philosophy was at length introduced among the Christians, but it was not always productive of the most salutary effects; knowledge was as often the parent of heresy as of devotion, and the description which was designed for the followers of Artemon may with equal propriety be applied to the various sects that resisted the successors of the apostles. "They presume to alter the holy scriptures, to abandon the ancient rule of faith, and to form their opinions according to the subtile precepts of logic. The science of the church is neglected for the study of geometry, and they lose sight of Heaven while they are employed in measuring the earth. Euclid is perpetually in their hands. Aristotle and Theophrastus are the objects of their admiration; and they express an uncommon reverence for the works of Galen. Their errors are derived from the abuse of the arts and sciences of the infidels, and they corrupt the simplicity of the Gospel by the refinements of human reason."

Nor can it be affirmed with truth that the advantages of birth and fortune were always separated from the profession of Christianity. Several Roman citizens were brought before the tribunal of Pliny, and he soon discovered that a great number of persons of *every order* of men in Bithynia had deserted the religion of their ancestors. His unsuspected testimony may, in this instance, obtain more credit than the bold challenge of Tertullian, when he addresses himself to the fears as well as to the humanity of the proconsul of Africa, by assuring him that, if he persists in his cruel intentions, he must decimate Carthage, and that he will find among the guilty many persons of his own rank, senators and matrons of noblest extraction, and the friends or relations of his most intimate friends. It appears, however, that about forty years afterwards the emperor Valerian was persuaded of the truth of this assertion, since in one of his rescripts he evidently supposes that senators, Roman knights, and ladies of quality were engaged in the Christian sect. The church still continued to increase its outward splendour as it lost its internal purity; and in the reign of Diocletian the palace, the courts of justice, and even the army concealed a multitude of Christians who endeavoured to reconcile the interests of the present with those of a future life.

And yet these exceptions are either too few in number, or too recent in time, entirely to remove the imputation of ignorance and obscurity which has been so arrogantly cast on the first proselytes of Christianity. Instead of employing in our defence the fictions of later ages, it will be more prudent to convert the occasion of scandal into a subject of edification. Our serious thoughts will suggest to us that the apostles themselves were chosen by providence among the fishermen of Galilee, and that, the lower we depress the temporal condition of the first Christians, the more reason we shall find to admire their merit and success. It is incumbent on us diligently to remember that the kingdom of heaven was promised to the poor in spirit, and that minds afflicted by calamity and the contempt of mankind cheerfully listen to the divine promise of future happiness; while, on the contrary, the fortunate are satisfied with the possession of this world; and the wise abuse in doubt and dispute their vain superiority of reason and knowledge.

We stand in need of such reflections to comfort us for the loss of some illustrious characters, which in our eyes might have seemed the most worthy of the heavenly present. The names of Seneca, of the elder and the younger Pliny, of Tacitus, of Plutarch, of Galen, of the slave Epictetus, and of the emperor Marcus Antoninus, adorn the age in which they flourished, and exalt the dignity of human nature. They filled with glory their respective stations, either in active or contemplative life; their excellent understandings were improved by study; Philosophy had purified their minds from the prejudices of the popular superstition; and their days were spent in the pursuit of truth and the practice of virtue. Yet all these sages (it is no less an object of surprise than of concern) overlooked or rejected the perfection of the Christian system. Their language or their silence equally discover their contempt for the growing sect, which in their time had diffused itself over the Roman empire. Those among them who condescend to mention the Christians consider them only as obstinate and perverse enthusiasts, who exacted an implicit submission to their mysterious doctrines, without being able to produce a single argument that could engage the attention of men of sense and learning.

It is at least doubtful whether any of these philosophers perused the apologies which the primitive Christians repeatedly published in behalf of themselves and of their religion; but it is much to be lamented that such a cause was not defended by abler advocates. They expose with superfluous wit and eloquence the extravagance of Polytheism. They interest our compassion by displaying the innocence and sufferings of their injured brethren. But, when they would demonstrate the divine origin of Christianity, they insist much more strongly on the predictions which announced, than on the miracles which accompanied, the appearance of the Messiah. Their favourite argument might serve to edify a Christian or to convert a Jew, since both the one and the other acknowledge the authority of those prophecies, and both are obliged, with devout reverence, to search for their sense and their accomplishment. But this mode of persuasion loses much of its weight and influence when it is addressed to those who neither understand nor respect the Mosaic dispensation and the prophetic style. In the unskilful hands of Justin and of the succeeding apologists, the sublime meaning of the Hebrew oracles evaporates in distant types, affected conceits, and cold allegories; and even their authenticity was rendered suspicious to an unenlightened Gentile by the mixture of pious forgeries, which, under the names of Orpheus, Hermes, and the Sibyls, were obtruded on him as of equal value with the genuine inspirations of Heaven. The adoption of fraud and sophistry in the defence of revelation too often reminds us of the injudicious conduct of those poets who load their *invulnerable* heroes with a useless weight of cumbersome and brittle armour.

But how shall we excuse the supine inattention of the Pagan and philosophic world to those evidences which were presented by the hand of Omnipotence, not to their reason, but to their senses? During the age of Christ, of his apostles, and of their first disciples, the doctrine which they preached was confirmed by innumerable prodigies. The lame walked, the blind saw, the sick were healed, the dead were raised, dæmons were expelled, and the laws of Nature were frequently suspended for the benefit of the church. But the sages of Greece and Rome turned aside from the awful spectacle, and, pursuing the ordinary occupations of life and study, appeared unconscious of any alterations in the moral or physical government of the world. Under the reign of Tiberius, the whole earth, or at least a celebrated province of the Roman empire, was involved in a præternatural darkness of three hours. Even this miraculous event, which ought to have excited the wonder, the curiosity, and the devotion of mankind, passed without notice in an age of science and history. It happened during the lifetime of Seneca and the elder Pliny, who must have experienced the immediate effects, or received the earliest intelligence, of the prodigy. Each of these philosophers, in a laborious work, has recorded all the great phenomena of Nature, earthquakes, meteors, comets, and eclipses, which his indefatigable curiosity could collect. Both the one and the other have omitted to mention the greatest phenomenon to which the mortal eye has been witness since the creation of the globe. A distinct chapter of Pliny is designed for eclipses of an extraordinary nature and unusual duration; but he contents himself with describing the singular defect of light which followed the murder of Cæsar, when, during the greatest part of the year, the orb of the sun appeared pale and without splendour. This season of obscurity, which cannot surely be compared with the præternatural darkness of the Passion, had been already celebrated by most of the poets and historians of that memorable age.

CHAPTER XVI

IF we seriously consider the purity of the Christian religion, the sanctity of its moral precepts, and the innocent as well as austere lives of the greater number of those who, during the first ages, embraced the faith of the gospel, we should naturally suppose that so benevolent a doctrine would have been received with due reverence even by the unbelieving world; that the learned and the polite, however they might deride the miracles, would have esteemed the virtues of the new sect; and that the magistrates, instead of persecuting, would have protected an order of men who yielded the most passive obedience to the laws, though they declined the active cares of war and government. If, on the other hand, we recollect the universal toleration of Polytheism, as it was invariably maintained by the faith of the people, the incredulity of philosophers, and the policy of the Roman senate and emperors, we are at a loss to discover what new offence the Christians had committed, what new provocation could exasperate the mild indifference of antiquity, and what new motives could urge the Roman princes, who beheld, without concern, a thousand forms of religion subsisting in peace under their gentle sway, to inflict a severe punishment on any part of their subjects, who had chosen for themselves a singular, but an inoffensive, mode of faith and worship.

The religious policy of the ancient world seems to have assumed a more stern and intolerant character, to oppose the progress of Christianity. About fourscore years after the death of Christ, his innocent disciples were punished with death, by the sentence of a proconsul of the most amiable and philosophic character, and according to the laws of an emperor distinguished by the wisdom and justice of his general administration. The apologies which were repeatedly addressed to the successors of Trajan are filled with the most pathetic complaints, that the Christians, who obeyed the dictates and solicited the liberty of conscience, were alone, among all the subjects of the Roman empire, excluded from the common benefits of their auspicious government. The deaths of a few eminent martyrs have been recorded with care; and from the time that Christianity was invested with the supreme power, the governors of the church have been no less diligently employed in displaying the cruelty than in imitating the conduct of their Pagan adversaries. To separate (if it be possible) a few authentic as well as interesting facts from an undigested mass of fiction and error, and to relate, in a clear and rational manner, the causes, the extent, the duration, and the most important circumstances of the persecutions to which the first Christians were exposed, is the design of the present Chapter.

The sectaries of a persecuted religion, depressed by fear, animated with resentment, and perhaps heated by enthusiasm, are seldom in a proper temper of mind calmly to investigate, or candidly to appreciate, the motives of their enemies, which often escape the impartial and discerning view even of those who are placed at a secure distance from the flames of persecution. A reason has been assigned for the conduct of the emperors towards the primitive Christians, which may appear the more specious and probable as it is drawn from the acknowledged genius of Polytheism. It has already been observed that the religious concord of the world was principally supported by the implicit assent and reverence which the nations of antiquity expressed for their respective traditions and ceremonies. It might therefore be expected that they would unite with indignation against any sect of people which should separate itself from the communion of mankind, and, claiming the exclusive possession of divine knowledge, should disdain every form of worship, except its own, as impious and idolatrous. The rights of toleration were held by mutual indulgence; they were justly forfeited by a refusal of the accustomed tribute. As the payment of this tribute was inflexibly refused by the Jews, and by them alone, the consideration of the treatment which they experienced from the Roman magistrates will serve to explain how far these speculations are justified by facts, and will lead us to discover the true causes of the persecution of Christianity.

Without repeating what has been already mentioned of the reverence of the Roman princes and governors for the temple of Jerusalem, we shall only observe that the destruction of the temple and city was accompanied and followed by every circumstance that could exasperate the minds of the conquerors, and authorize religious persecution by the most specious arguments of political justice and the public safety. From the reign of Nero to that of Antoninus Pius, the Jews discovered a fierce impatience of the dominion of Rome, which repeatedly broke out in the most furious massacres and insurrections. Humanity is shocked at the recital of the horrid cruelties which they committed in the cities of Egypt, of Cyprus, and of Cyrene, where they dwelt in treacherous friendship with the unsuspecting natives; and we are tempted to applaud the severe retaliation which was exercised by the arms of the legions against a race of fanatics, whose dire and credulous superstition seemed to render them the implacable enemies not only of the Roman government, but of human kind. The enthusiasm of the Jews was supported by the opinion that it was unlawful for them to pay taxes to an idolatrous master; and by the flattering promise which they derived from their ancient oracles, that a conquering Messiah would soon arise, destined to break their fetters and to invest the favourites of heaven with the empire of the earth. It was by announcing himself as their long-expected deliverer, and by calling on all the descendants of Abraham to assert the hope of Israel, that the famous Barchochebas collected a formidable army, with which he resisted, during two years, the power of the emperor Hadrian.

Notwithstanding these repeated provocations, the resentment of the Roman princes expired after the victory; nor were their apprehensions continued beyond the period of war and danger. By the general indulgence of polytheism, and by the mild temper of Antoninus Pius, the Jews were restored to their ancient privileges, and once more obtained the permission of circumcising their children, with the easy restraint that they should never confer on any foreign proselyte that distinguishing mark of the Hebrew race. The numerous remains of that people, though they were still excluded from the precincts of Jerusalem, were permitted to form and to maintain considerable establishments both in Italy and in the provinces, to acquire the freedom of Rome, to enjoy municipal honours, and to obtain, at the same time, an exemption from the burdensome and expensive offices of society. The moderation or the contempt of the Romans gave a legal sanction to the form of ecclesiastical police which was instituted by the vanquished sect. The patriarch, who had fixed his residence at Tiberias, was empowered to appoint his subordinate ministers and apostles, to exercise a domestic jurisdiction, and to receive from his dispersed brethren an annual contribution. New synagogues were frequently erected in the principal cities of the empire; and the sabbaths, the fasts, and the festivals, which were either commanded by the Mosaic laws or enjoined by the traditions of the Rabbis, were celebrated in the most solemn and public manner. Such gentle treatment insensibly assuaged the stern temper of the Jews. Awakened from their dream of prophecy and conquest, they assumed the behaviour of peaceable and industrious subjects. Their irreconcileable hatred of mankind, instead of flaming out in acts of blood and violence, evaporated in less dangerous gratifications. They embraced every opportunity of over-reaching the idolaters in trade; and they pronounced secret and ambiguous imprecations against the haughty kingdom of Edom.

Since the Jews, who rejected with abhorrence the deities adored by their sovereign and by their fellow-subjects, enjoyed, however, the free exercise of their unsocial religion, there must have existed some other cause which exposed the disciples of Christ to those severities from which the posterity of Abraham was exempt. The difference between them is simple and obvious; but, according to the sentiments of antiquity, it was of the highest importance. The Jews were a *nation;* the Christians were a *sect;* and, if it was natural for every community to respect the sacred institutions of their neighbours, it was incumbent on them to persevere in those of their ancestors. The voice of oracles, the precepts of philosophers and the authority of the laws unanimously enforced this national obligation. By their lofty claim of superior sanctity, the Jews might provoke the Polytheists to consider them as an odious and impure race. By disdaining the intercourse of other nations they might deserve their contempt. The laws of Moses might be for the most part frivolous or absurd; yet, since they had been received during many ages by a large society, his followers were justified by the example of mankind; and it was universally acknowledged that they had a right to practise what it would have been criminal in them to neglect. But this principle which protected the Jewish synagogue afforded not any favour or security to the primitive church. By embracing the faith of the Gospel, the Christians incurred the supposed guilt of an unnatural and unpardonable offence. They dissolved the sacred ties of custom and education, violated the religious institutions of their country, and presumptuously despised whatever their fathers had believed as true, or had reverenced as sacred. Nor was this apostacy (if we may use the expression) merely of a partial or local kind; since the pious deserter who withdrew himself from the temples of Egypt or Syria would equally disdain to seek an asylum in those of Athens or Carthage. Every Christian rejected with contempt the superstitions of his family, his city, and his province. The whole body of Christians unanimously refused to hold any communion with the gods of Rome, of the empire, and of mankind. It was in vain that the oppressed believer asserted the inalienable rights of conscience and private judgment. Though his situation might excite the pity, his arguments could never reach the understanding, either of the philosophic or of the believing part of the Pagan world. To their apprehensions, it was no less a matter of surprise that any individuals should entertain scruples against complying with the established mode of worship, than if they had conceived a sudden abhorrence to the manners, the dress, or the language of their native country.

The surprise of the Pagans was soon succeeded by resentment; and the most pious of men were exposed to the unjust but dangerous imputation of impiety. Malice and prejudice concurred in representing the Christians as a society of atheists, who, by the most daring attack on the religious constitution of the empire, had merited the severest animadversion of the civil magistrate. They had separated themselves (they gloried in the confession) from every mode of superstition which was received in any part of the globe by the various temper of polytheism; but it was not altogether so evident what deity or what form of worship they had substituted to the gods and temples of antiquity. The pure and sublime idea which they entertained of the Supreme Being escaped the gross conception of the Pagan multitude, who were at a loss to discover a spiritual and solitary God that was neither represented under any corporeal figure or visible symbol, nor was adored with the accustomed pomp of libations and festivals, of altars and sacrifices. The sages of Greece and Rome, who had elevated their minds to the contemplation of the existence and attributes of the First Cause, were induced, by reason or by vanity, to reserve for themselves and their chosen disciples the privilege of this philosophical devotion. They were far from admitting the prejudices of mankind as the standard of truth; but they considered them as flowing from the original disposition of human nature; and they supposed that any popular mode of faith and worship which presumed to disclaim the assistance of the senses would, in proportion as it receded from superstition, find itself incapable of restraining the wanderings of the fancy and the visions of fanaticism. The careless glance which men of wit and learning condescended to cast on the Christian revelation served only to confirm their hasty opinion, and to persuade them that the principle, which they might have revered, of the divine unity was defaced by the wild enthusiasm, and annihilated by the airy speculations, of the new sectaries. The author of a celebrated dialogue which has been attributed to Lucian, whilst he affects to treat the mysterious subject of the Trinity in a style of ridicule and contempt, betrays his own ignorance of the weakness of human reason, and of the inscrutable nature of the divine perfections.

It might appear less surprising that the founder of Christianity should not only be revered by his disciples as a sage and a prophet, but should be adored as a God. The Polytheists were disposed to adopt every article of faith which seemed to offer any resemblance, however distant or imperfect, with the popular mythology; and the legends of Bacchus, of Hercules, and of Æsculapius, had in some measure prepared their imagination for the appearance of the Son of God under a human form. But they were astonished that the Christians should abandon the temples of those ancient heroes who, in the infancy of the world, had invented arts, instituted laws, and vanquished the tyrants or monsters who infested the earth, in order to choose, for the exclusive object of their religious worship, an obscure teacher who, in a recent age, and among a barbarous people, had fallen a sacrifice either to the malice of his own countrymen or to the jealousy of the Roman government. The Pagan multitude, reserving their gratitude for temporal benefits alone, rejected the inestimable present of life and immortality which was offered to mankind by Jesus of Nazareth. His mild constancy in the midst of cruel and voluntary sufferings, his universal benevolence, and the sublime simplicity of his actions and character, were insufficient, in the opinion of those carnal men, to compensate for the want of fame, of empire, and of success; and, whilst they refused to acknowledge his stupendous triumph over the powers of darkness and of the grave, they misrepresented, or they insulted, the equivocal birth, wandering life, and ignominious death of the divine Author of Christianity.

The personal guilt which every Christian had contracted, in thus preferring his private sentiment to the national religion, was aggravated, in a very high degree, by the number and union of the criminals.   It is well known, and has been already observed, that Roman policy viewed with the utmost jealousy and distrust any association among its subjects, and that the privileges of private corporations, though formed for the most harmless or beneficial purposes, were bestowed with a very sparing hand.   The religious assemblies of the Christians, who had separated themselves from the public worship, appeared of a much less innocent nature; they were illegal in their principle, and in their consequences might become dangerous; nor were the emperors conscious that they violated the laws of justice, when, for the peace of society, they prohibited those secret and sometimes nocturnal meetings.   The pious disobedience of the Christians made their conduct, or perhaps their designs, appear in a much more serious and criminal light; and the Roman princes, who might perhaps have suffered themselves to be disarmed by a ready submission, deeming their honour concerned in the execution of their commands, sometimes attempted by rigorous punishments to subdue this independent spirit, which boldly acknowledged an authority superior to that of the magistrate.   The extent and duration of this spiritual conspiracy seemed to render it every day more deserving of his animadversion.   We have already seen that the active and successful zeal of the Christians had insensibly diffused them through every province and almost every city of the empire. The new converts seemed to renounce their family and country, that they might connect themselves in an indissoluble band of union with a peculiar society, which everywhere assumed a different character from the rest of mankind. Their gloomy and austere aspect, their abhorrence of the common business and pleasures of life, and their frequent predictions of impending calamities, inspired the Pagans with the apprehension of some danger which would arise from the new sect, the more alarming as it was the more obscure. "Whatever," says Pliny, "may be the principle of their conduct, their inflexible obstinacy appeared deserving of punishment."

The precautions with which the disciples of Christ performed the offices of religion were at first dictated by fear and necessity; but they were continued from choice. By imitating the awful secrecy which reigned in the Eleusinian mysteries, the Christians had flattered themselves that they should render their sacred institutions more respectable in the eyes of the Pagan world. But the event, as it often happens to the operations of subtile policy, deceived their wishes and their expectations. It was concluded that they only concealed what they would have blushed to disclose. Their mistaken prudence afforded an opportunity for malice to invent, and for suspicious credulity to believe, the horrid tales which described the Christians as the most wicked of human kind, who practised in their dark recesses every abomination that a depraved fancy could suggest, and who solicited the favour of their unknown God by the sacrifice of every moral virtue. There were many who pretended to confess or to relate the ceremonies of this abhorred society. It was asserted "that a new-born infant, entirely covered over with flour, was presented, like some mystic symbol of initiation, to the knife of the pro-selyte, who unknowingly inflicted many a secret and mortal wound on the innocent victim of his error; that, as soon as the cruel deed was perpetrated, the sectaries drank up the blood, greedily tore asunder the quivering members, and pledged themselves to eternal secrecy, by a mutual consciousness of guilt. It was as confidently affirmed that this inhuman sacrifice was succeeded by a suitable entertainment, in which intemperance served as a provocative to brutal lust; till, at the appointed moment, the lights were suddenly extinguished, shame was banished, nature was forgotten; and, as accident might direct, the darkness of the night was polluted by the incestuous commerce of sisters and brothers, of sons and of mothers."

But the perusal of the ancient apologies was sufficient to remove even the slightest suspicion from the mind of a candid adversary. The Christians, with the intrepid security of innocence, appeal from the voice of rumour to the equity of the magistrates. They acknowledge that, if any proof can be produced of the crimes which calumny has imputed to them, they are worthy of the most severe punishment. They provoke the punishment, and they challenge the proof. At the same time they urge, with equal truth and propriety, that the charge is not less devoid of probability than it is destitute of evidence; they ask whether any one can seriously believe that the pure and holy precepts of the Gospel, which so frequently restrain the use of the most lawful enjoyments, should inculcate the practice of the most abominable crimes; that a large society should resolve to dishonour itself in the eyes of its own members; and that a great number of persons of either sex, and every age and character, insensible to the fear of death or infamy, should consent to violate those principles which nature and education had imprinted most deeply in their minds. Nothing, it should seem, could weaken the force or destroy the effect of so unanswerable a justification, unless it were the injudicious conduct of the apologists themselves, who betrayed the common cause of religion, to gratify their devout hatred to the domestic enemies of the church. It was sometimes faintly insinuated, and sometimes boldly asserted, that the same bloody sacrifices, and the same incestuous festivals, which were so falsely ascribed to the orthodox believers, were in reality celebrated by the Marcionites, by the Carpocratians, and by several other sects of the Gnostics, who, notwithstanding they might deviate into the paths of heresy, were still actuated by the sentiments of men, and still governed by the precepts of Christianity. Accusations of a similar kind were retorted upon the church by the schismatics who had departed from its communion; and it was confessed on all sides that the most scandalous licentiousness of manners prevailed among great numbers of those who affected the name of Christians. A Pagan magistrate, who possessed neither leisure nor abilities to discern the almost imperceptible line which divides the orthodox faith from heretical pravity, might easily have imagined that their mutual animosity had extorted the discovery of their common guilt. It was fortunate for the repose, or at least for the reputation, of the first Christians, that the magistrates sometimes proceeded with more temper and moderation than is usually consistent with religious zeal, and that they reported, as the impartial result of their judicial inquiry, that the sectaries who had deserted the established worship appeared to them sincere in their professions and blameless in their manners; however they might incur, by their absurd and excessive superstition, the censure of the laws.

History, which undertakes to record the transactions of the past for the instruction of future ages, would ill deserve that honourable office, if she condescended to plead the cause of tyrants, or to justify the maxims of persecution. It must, however, be acknowledged that the conduct of the emperors who appeared the least favourable to the primitive church is by no means so criminal as that of modern sovereigns who have employed the arm of violence and terror against the religious opinions of any part of their subjects. From their reflections, or even from their own feelings, a Charles V. or a Louis XIV. might have acquired a just knowledge of the rights of conscience, of the obligation of faith, and of the innocence of error. But the princes and magistrates of ancient Rome were strangers to those principles which inspired and authorized the inflexible obstinacy of the Christians in the cause of truth, nor could they themselves discover in their own breasts any motive which would have prompted them to refuse a legal, and as it were a natural, submission to the sacred institutions of their country. The same reason which contributes to alleviate the guilt, must have tended to abate the rigour, of their persecutions. As they were actuated not by the furious zeal of bigots, but by the temperate policy of legislators, contempt must often have relaxed, and humanity must frequently have suspended, the execution of those laws which they enacted against the humble and obscure followers of Christ. From the general view of their character and motives we might naturally conclude : I. That a considerable time elapsed before they considered the new sectaries as an object deserving of the attention of government. II. That, in the conviction of any of their subjects who were accused of so very singular a crime, they proceeded with caution and reluctance. III. That they were moderate in the use of punishments; and IV. That the afflicted church enjoyed many intervals of peace and tranquillity. Notwithstanding the careless indifference which the most copious and the most minute of the Pagan writers have shewn to the affairs of the Christians, it may still be in our power to confirm each of these probable suppositions by the evidence of authentic facts.

I. By the wise dispensation of Providence, a mysterious veil was cast over the infancy of the church, which, till the faith of the Christians was matured and their numbers were multiplied, served to protect them not only from the malice, but even from the knowledge, of the Pagan world. The slow and gradual abolition of the Mosaic ceremonies afforded a safe and innocent disguise to the more early proselytes of the Gospel. As they were for the greater part of the race of Abraham, they were distinguished by the peculiar mark of circumcision, offered up their devotions in the Temple of Jerusalem till its final destruction, and received both the Law and the Prophets as the genuine inspirations of the Deity. The Gentile converts, who by a spiritual adoption had been associated to the hope of Israel, were likewise confounded under the garb and appearance of Jews, and, as the Polytheists paid less regard to articles of faith than to the external worship, the new sect, which carefully concealed, or faintly announced, its future greatness and ambition, was permitted to shelter itself under the general toleration which was granted to an ancient and celebrated people in the Roman empire. It was not long, perhaps, before the Jews themselves, animated with a fiercer zeal and a more jealous faith, perceived the gradual separation of their Nazarene brethren from the doctrine of the synagogue; and they would gladly have extinguished the dangerous heresy in the blood of its adherents. But the decrees of heaven had already disarmed their malice; and, though they might sometimes exert the licentious privilege of sedition, they no longer possessed the administration of criminal justice; nor did they find it easy to infuse into the calm breast of a Roman magistrate the rancour of their own zeal and prejudice. The provincial governors declared themselves ready to listen to any accusation that might affect the public safety; but, as soon as they were informed that it was a question not of facts but of words, a dispute relating only to the interpretation of the Jewish laws and prophecies, they deemed it unworthy of the majesty of Rome seriously to discuss the obscure differences which might arise among a barbarous and superstitious people. The innocence of the first Christians was protected by ignorance and contempt; and the tribunal of the Pagan magistrate often proved their most assured refuge against the fury of the synagogue. If, indeed, we were disposed to adopt the traditions of a too credulous antiquity, we might relate the distant peregrinations, the wonderful achievements, and the various deaths, of the twelve apostles; but a more accurate inquiry will induce us to doubt whether any of those persons who had been witnesses to the miracles of Christ were permitted, beyond the limits of Palestine, to seal with their blood the truth of their testimony. From the ordinary term of human life, it may very naturally be presumed that most of them were deceased before the discontent of the Jews broke out into that furious war which was terminated only by the ruin of Jerusalem. During a long period, from the death of Christ to that memorable rebellion, we cannot discover any traces of Roman intolerance, unless they are to be found in the sudden, the transient, but the cruel persecution, which was exercised by Nero against the Christians of the capital, thirty-five years after the former, and only two years before the latter of those great events. The character of the philosophic historian, to whom we are principally indebted for the knowledge of this singular transaction, would alone be sufficient to recommend it to our most attentive consideration.

In the tenth year of the reign of Nero, the capital of the empire was afflicted by a fire which raged beyond the memory or example of former ages. The monuments of Grecian art and of Roman virtue, the trophies of the Punic and Gallic wars, the most holy temples, and the most splendid palaces, were involved in one common destruction. Of the fourteen regions or quarters into which Rome was divided, four only subsisted entire, three were levelled with the ground, and the remaining seven which had experienced the fury of the flames displayed a melancholy prospect of ruin and desolation. The vigilance of government appears not to have neglected any of the precautions which might alleviate the sense of so dreadful a calamity. The Imperial gardens were thrown open to the distressed multitude, temporary buildings were erected for their accommodation, and a plentiful supply of corn and provisions was distributed at a very moderate price. The most generous policy seemed to have dictated the edicts which regulated the disposition of the streets and the construction of private houses; and, as it usually happens in an age of prosperity, the conflagration of Rome, in the course of a few years, produced a new city, more regular and more beautiful than the former. But all the prudence and humanity affected by Nero on this occasion were insufficient to preserve him from the popular suspicion. Every crime might be imputed to the assassin of his wife and mother; nor could the prince who prostituted his person and dignity on the theatre be deemed incapable of the most extravagant folly. The voice of rumour accused the emperor as the incendiary of his own capital; and, as the most incredible stories are the best adapted to the genius of an enraged people, it was gravely reported, and firmly believed, that Nero, enjoying the calamity which he had occasioned, amused himself with singing to his lyre the destruction of ancient Troy. To divert a suspicion which the power of despotism was unable to suppress, the emperor resolved to substitute in his own place some fictitious criminals. " With this view (continues Tacitus) he inflicted the most exquisite tortures on those men, who, under the vulgar appellation of Christians, were already branded with deserved infamy. They derived their name and origin from Christ, who, in the reign of Tiberius, had suffered death by the sentence of the procurator Pontius Pilate. For a while this dire superstition was checked; but it again burst forth, and not only spread itself over Judæa, the first seat of this mischievous sect, but was even introduced into Rome, the common asylum which receives and protects whatever is impure, whatever is atrocious. The confessions of those who were seized, discovered a great multitude of their accomplices, and they were all convicted, not so much for the crime of setting fire to the city, as for their hatred of human kind. They died in torments, and their torments were embittered by insult and derision. Some were nailed on crosses; others sewn up in the skins of wild beasts, and exposed to the fury of dogs;

others again, smeared over with combustible materials, were used as torches to illuminate the darkness of the night. The gardens of Nero were destined for the melancholy spectacle, which was accompanied with a horse race, and honoured with the presence of the emperor, who mingled with the populace in the dress and attitude of a charioteer. The guilt of the Christians deserved, indeed, the most exemplary punishment, but the public abhorrence was changed into commiseration, from the opinion that those unhappy wretches were sacrificed not so much to the public welfare as to the cruelty of a jealous tyrant." Those who survey with a curious eye the revolutions of mankind may observe that the gardens and circus of Nero on the Vatican, which were polluted with the blood of the first Christians, have been rendered still more famous by the triumph and by the abuse of the persecuted religion. On the same spot, a temple which far surpasses the ancient glories of the Capitol has been since erected by the Christian Pontiffs, who, deriving their claim of universal dominion from an humble fisherman of Galilee, have succeeded to the throne of the Cæsars, given laws to the barbarian conquerors of Rome, and extended their spiritual jurisdiction from the coast of the Baltic to the shores of the Pacific Ocean.

But it would be improper to dismiss this account of Nero's persecution till we have made some observations that may serve to remove the difficulties with which it is perplexed and to throw some light on the subsequent history of the church.

1. The most sceptical criticism is obliged to respect the truth of this extraordinary fact, and the integrity of this celebrated passage of Tacitus. The former is confirmed by the diligent and accurate Suetonius, who mentions the punishment which Nero inflicted on the Christians, a sect of men who had embraced a new and criminal superstition. The latter may be proved by the consent of the most ancient manuscripts; by the inimitable character of the style of Tacitus; by his reputation, which guarded his text from the inter-

polations of pious fraud; and by the purport of his
narration, which accused the first Christians of the
most atrocious crimes, without insinuating that they
possessed any miraculous or even magical powers
above the rest of mankind.   2. Notwithstanding it is
probable that Tacitus was born some years before the
fire of Rome, he could derive only from reading and
conversation the knowledge of an event which happened during his infancy.   Before he gave himself
to the Public, he calmly waited till his genius had
attained its full maturity, and he was more than forty
years of age when a grateful regard for the memory
of the virtuous Agricola extorted from him the most
early of those historical compositions which will delight
and instruct the most distant posterity.   After making
a trial of his strength in the life of Agricola and the
description of Germany, he conceived, and at length
executed, a more arduous work, the history of Rome,
in thirty books, from the fall of Nero to the accession
of Nerva.   The administration of Nerva introduced
an age of justice and prosperity, which Tacitus had
destined for the occupation of his old age; but, when
he took a nearer view of his subject, judging perhaps
that it was a more honourable or a less invidious office
to record the vices of past tyrants than to celebrate
the virtues of a reigning monarch, he chose rather to
relate, under the form of annals, the actions of the
four immediate successors of Augustus.   To collect,
to dispose, and to adorn a series of fourscore years in
an immortal work, every sentence of which is pregnant
with the deepest observations and the most lively
images, was an undertaking sufficient to exercise the
genius of Tacitus himself during the greatest part of
his life.   In the last years of the reign of Trajan, whilst
the victorious monarch extended the power of Rome
beyond its ancient limits, the historian was describing,
in the second and fourth books of his annals, the
tyranny of Tiberius; and the emperor Hadrian must
have succeeded to the throne before Tacitus, in the
regular prosecution of his work, could relate the fire
of the capital and the cruelty of Nero towards the

unfortunate Christians. At the distance of sixty years, it was the duty of the annalist to adopt the narratives of contemporaries; but it was natural for the philosopher to indulge himself in the description of the origin, the progress, and the character of the new sect, not so much according to the knowledge or prejudices of the age of Nero, as according to those of the time of Hadrian. 3. Tacitus very frequently trusts to the curiosity or reflection of his readers to supply those intermediate circumstances and ideas which, in his extreme conciseness, he has thought proper to suppress. We may therefore presume to imagine some probable cause which could direct the cruelty of Nero against the Christians of Rome, whose obscurity, as well as innocence, should have shielded them from his indignation, and even from his notice. The Jews, who were numerous in the capital, and oppressed in their own country, were a much fitter object for the suspicions of the emperor and of the people; nor did it seem unlikely that a vanquished nation, who already discovered their abhorrence of the Roman yoke, might have recourse to the most atrocious means of gratifying their implacable revenge. But the Jews possessed very powerful advocates in the palace, and even in the heart of the tyrant; his wife and mistress, the beautiful Poppæa, and a favourite player of the race of Abraham, who had already employed their intercession in behalf of the obnoxious people. In their room it was necessary to offer some other victims, and it might easily be suggested, that, although the genuine followers of Moses were innocent of the fire of Rome, there had arisen among them a new and pernicious sect of GALILÆANS, which was capable of the most horrid crimes. Under the appellation of GALILÆANS, two distinctions of men were confounded, the most opposite to each other in their manners and principles; the disciples who had embraced the faith of Jesus of Nazareth, and the zealots who had followed the standard of Judas the Gaulonite. The former were the friends, and the latter were the enemies, of human kind; and the only resemblance between them consisted in the same inflexible constancy which, in the defence of their cause, rendered them insensible of death and tortures. The followers of Judas, who impelled their countrymen into rebellion, were soon buried under the ruins of Jerusalem; whilst those of Jesus, known by the more celebrated name of Christians, diffused themselves over the Roman empire. How natural was it for Tacitus, in the time of Hadrian, to appropriate to the Christians the guilt and the sufferings which he might, with far greater truth and justice, have attributed to a sect whose odious memory was almost extinguished ! 4. Whatever opinion may be entertained of this conjecture (for it is no more than a conjecture), it is evident that the effect, as well as the cause, of Nero's persecution were confined to the walls of Rome; that the religious tenets of the Galilæans, or Christians, were never made a subject of punishment or even of inquiry; and that, as the idea of their sufferings was for a long time connected with the idea of cruelty and injustice, the moderation of succeeding princes inclined them to spare a sect oppressed by a tyrant whose rage had been usually directed against virtue and innocence.

It is somewhat remarkable that the flames of war consumed almost at the same time the temple of Jerusalem and the Capitol of Rome; and it appears no less singular that the tribute which devotion had destined to the former should have been converted by the power of an assaulting victor to restore and adorn the splendour of the latter. The emperors levied a general capitation tax on the Jewish people; and, although the sum assessed on the head of each individual was inconsiderable, the use for which it was designed, and the severity with which it was exacted, were considered as an intolerable grievance. Since the officers of the revenue extended their unjust claim to many persons who were strangers to the blood or religion of the Jews, it was impossible that the Christians, who had so often sheltered themselves under the shade of the synagogue, should now escape this rapacious persecution. Anxious as they were to avoid the

slightest infection of idolatry, their conscience for-
bade them to contribute to the honour of that dæmon
who had assumed the character of the Capitoline
Jupiter.   As a very numerous, though declining, party
among the Christians still adhered to the law of Moses,
their efforts to dissemble their Jewish origin were
detected by the decisive test of circumcision, nor were
the Roman magistrates at leisure to inquire into the
difference of their religious tenets.   Among the
Christians who were brought before the tribunal of the
emperor, or, as it seems more probable, before that of
the procurator of Judæa, two persons are said to have
appeared, distinguished by their extraction, which was
more truly noble than that of the greatest monarchs.
These were the grandsons of St. Jude the apostle, who
himself was the brother of Jesus Christ.   Their natural
pretensions to the throne of David might perhaps
attract the respect of the people, and excite the
jealousy of the governor; but the meanness of their
garb and the simplicity of their answers soon convinced
him that they were neither desirous nor capable of
disturbing the peace of the Roman empire.   They
frankly confessed their royal origin and their near
relation to the Messiah; but they disclaimed any
temporal views, and professed that his kingdom, which
they devoutly expected, was purely of a spiritual and
angelic nature.   When they were examined concerning their fortune and occupation, they shewed their
hands hardened with daily labour, and declared that
they derived their whole subsistence from the cultiva-
tion of a farm near the village of Cocaba, of the extent
of about twenty-four English acres, and of the value of
nine thousand drachms, or three hundred pounds
sterling.   The grandsons of St. Jude were dismissed
with compassion and contempt.

But, although the obscurity of the house of David
might protect them from the suspicions of a tyrant,
the present greatness of his own family alarmed the
pusillanimous temper of Domitian, which could only
be appeased by the blood of those Romans whom he
either feared, or hated, or esteemed.   Of the two sons

of his uncle Flavius Sabinus, the elder was soon convicted of treasonable intentions, and the younger, who bore the name of Flavius Clemens, was indebted for his safety to his want of courage and ability. The emperor, for a long time, distinguished so harmless a kinsman by his favour and protection, bestowed on him his own niece Domitilla, adopted the children of that marriage to the hope of the succession, and invested their father with the honours of the consulship. But he had scarcely finished the term of his annual magistracy when, on a slight pretence, he was condemned and executed; Domitilla was banished to a desolate island on the coast of Campania; and sentences either of death or of confiscation were pronounced against a great number of persons who were involved in the same accusation. The guilt imputed to their charge was that of *Atheism* and *Jewish manners;* a singular association of ideas, which cannot with any propriety be applied except to the Christians, as they were obscurely and imperfectly viewed by the magistrates and by the writers of that period. On the strength of so probable an interpretation, and too eagerly admitting the suspicions of a tyrant as an evidence of their honourable crime, the church has placed both Clemens and Domitilla among its first martyrs, and has branded the cruelty of Domitian with the name of the second persecution. But this persecution (if it deserves that epithet) was of no long duration. A few months after the death of Clemens and the banishment of Domitilla, Stephen, a freedman belonging to the latter, who had enjoyed the favour but who had not surely embraced the faith of his mistress, assassinated the emperor in his palace. The memory of Domitian was condemned by the senate; his acts were rescinded; his exiles recalled; and under the gentle administration of Nerva, while the innocent were restored to their rank and fortunes, even the most guilty either obtained pardon or escaped punishment.

II. About ten years afterwards, under the reign of Trajan, the younger Pliny was intrusted by his friend and master with the government of Bithynia and

Pontus. He soon found himself at a loss to determine by what rule of justice or of law he should direct his conduct in the execution of an office the most repugnant to his humanity. Pliny had never assisted at any judicial proceedings against the Christians, with whose name alone he seems to be acquainted; and he was totally uninformed with regard to the nature of their guilt, the method of their conviction, and the degree of their punishment. In this perplexity he had recourse to his usual expedient, of submitting to the wisdom of Trajan an impartial and, in some respects, a favourable account of the new superstition, requesting the emperor that he would condescend to resolve his doubts and to instruct his ignorance. The life of Pliny had been employed in the acquisition of learning, and in the business of the world. Since the age of nineteen he had pleaded with distinction in the tribunals of Rome, filled a place in the senate, had been invested with the honours of the consulship, and had formed very numerous connexions with every order of men, both in Italy and in the provinces. From *his* ignorance, therefore, we may derive some useful information. We may assure ourselves that when he accepted the government of Bithynia there were no general laws or decrees of the senate in force against the Christians; that neither Trajan nor any of his virtuous predecessors, whose edicts were received into the civil and criminal jurisprudence, had publicly declared their intentions concerning the new sect; and that, whatever proceedings had been carried on against the Christians, there were none of sufficient weight and authority to establish a precedent for the conduct of a Roman magistrate.

The answer of Trajan, to which the Christians of the succeeding age have frequently appealed, discovers as much regard for justice and humanity as could be reconciled with his mistaken notions of religious policy. Instead of displaying the implacable zeal of an inquisitor, anxious to discover the most minute particles of heresy and exulting in the number of his victims, the emperor expresses much more solicitude to protect the security of the innocent than to prevent the escape of the guilty. He acknowledges the difficulty of fixing any general plan; but he lays down two salutary rules, which often afforded relief and support to the distressed Christians. Though he directs the magistrates to punish such persons as are legally convicted, he prohibits them, with a very humane inconsistency, from making any inquiries concerning the supposed criminals. Nor was the magistrate allowed to proceed on every kind of information. Anonymous charges the emperor rejects, as too repugnant to the equity of his government; and he strictly requires, for the conviction of those to whom the guilt of Christianity is imputed, the positive evidence of a fair and open accuser. It is likewise probable that the persons who assumed so invidious an office were obliged to declare the grounds of their suspicions, to specify (both in respect to time and place) the secret assemblies which their Christian adversary had frequented, and to disclose a great number of circumstances which were concealed with the most vigilant jealousy from the eye of the profane. If they succeeded in their prosecution, they were exposed to the resentment of a considerable and active party, to the censure of the more liberal portion of mankind, and to the ignominy which, in every age and country, has attended the character of an informer. If, on the contrary, they failed in their proofs, they incurred the severe, and perhaps capital, penalty which according to a law published by the emperor Hadrian was inflicted on those who falsely attributed to their fellow-citizens the crime of Christianity. The violence of personal or superstitious animosity might sometimes prevail over the most natural apprehensions of disgrace and danger; but it cannot surely be imagined that accusations of so unpromising an appearance were either lightly or frequently undertaken by the Pagan subjects of the Roman empire.

The expedient which was employed to elude the prudence of the laws affords a sufficient proof how effectually they disappointed the mischievous designs of private malice or superstitious zeal. In a large and tumultuous assembly, the restraints of fear and shame, so forcible on the minds of individuals, are deprived of the greatest part of their influence. The pious Christian, as he was desirous to obtain or to escape the glory of martyrdom, expected, either with impatience or with terror, the stated returns of the public games and festivals. On those occasions, the inhabitants of the great cities of the empire were collected in the circus of the theatre, where every circumstance of the place, as well as of the ceremony, contributed to kindle their devotion and to extinguish their humanity. Whilst the numerous spectators, crowned with garlands, perfumed with incense, purified with the blood of victims, and surrounded with the altars and statues of their tutelar deities, resigned themselves to the enjoyment of pleasures which they considered as an essential part of their religious worship, they recollected that the Christians alone abhorred the gods of mankind, and by their absence and melancholy on these solemn festivals seemed to insult or to lament the public felicity. If the empire had been afflicted by any recent calamity, by a plague, a famine, or an unsuccessful war; if the Tiber had, or if the Nile had not, risen beyond its banks; if the earth had shaken, or if the temperate order of the seasons had been interrupted, the superstitious Pagans were convinced that the crimes and the impiety of the Christians, who were spared by the excessive lenity of the government, had at length provoked the Divine Justice. It was not among a licentious and exasperated populace that the forms of legal proceedings could be observed; it was not in an amphitheatre, stained with the blood of wild beasts and gladiators, that the voice of compassion could be heard. The impatient clamours of the multitude denounced the Christians as the enemies of gods and men, doomed them to the severest tortures, and, venturing to accuse by name some of the most distinguished of the new sectaries, required, with irresistible vehemence, that they should be instantly apprehended and cast to the lions. The provincial governors and magistrates who presided in the public spectacles were usually inclined to gratify the inclinations, and to appease the rage, of the people by the sacrifice of a few obnoxious victims. But the wisdom of the emperors protected the church from the danger of these tumultuous clamours and irregular accusations, which they justly censured as repugnant both to the firmness and to the equity of their administration. The edicts of Hadrian and of Antoninus Pius expressly declared that the voice of the multitude should never be admitted as legal evidence to convict or to punish those unfortunate persons who had embraced the enthusiasm of the Christians.

III. Punishment was not the inevitable consequence of conviction, and the Christians whose guilt was the most clearly proved by the testimony of witnesses, or even by their voluntary confession, still retained in their own power the alternative of life or death. It was not so much the past offence, as the actual resistance, which excited the indignation of the magistrate. He was persuaded that he offered them an easy pardon, since, if they consented to cast a few grains of incense upon the altar, they were dismissed from the tribunal in safety and with applause. It was esteemed the duty of a humane judge to endeavour to reclaim, rather than to punish, those deluded enthusiasts. Varying his tone according to the age, the sex, or the situation of the prisoners, he frequently condescended to set before their eyes every circumstance which could render life more pleasing, or death more terrible; and to solicit, nay, to intreat them, that they would show some compassion to themselves, to their families, and to their friends. If threats and persuasions proved ineffectual, he had often recourse to violence; the scourge and the rack were called in to supply the deficiency of argument, and every art of cruelty was employed to subdue such inflexible and, as it appeared to the Pagans, such criminal obstinacy. The ancient apologists of Christianity have censured, with equal truth and severity, the irregular conduct of their persecutors, who, contrary to every principle of judicial proceeding, admitted the use of torture, in order to obtain not a confession but a denial of the crime which was the object of their inquiry. The monks of succeeding ages, who, in their peaceful solitudes, entertained themselves with diversifying the death and sufferings of the primitive martyrs, have frequently invented torments of a much more refined and ingenious nature. In particular, it has pleased them to suppose that the zeal of the Roman magistrates, disdaining every consideration of moral virtue or public decency, endeavoured to seduce those whom they were unable to vanquish, and that, by their orders, the most brutal violence was offered to those whom they found it impossible to seduce. It is related that pious females, who were prepared to despise death, were sometimes condemned to a more severe trial, and called upon to determine whether they set a higher value on their religion or on their chastity. The youths to whose licentious embraces they were abandoned received a solemn exhortation from the judge to exert their most strenuous efforts to maintain the honour of Venus against the impious virgin who refused to burn incense on her altars. Their violence, however, was commonly disappointed; and the seasonable interposition of some miraculous power preserved the chaste spouses of Christ from the dishonour even of an involuntary defeat. We should not, indeed, neglect to remark that the more ancient, as well as authentic, memorials of the church are seldom polluted with these extravagant and indecent fictions.

The total disregard of truth and probability in the representation of these primitive martyrdoms was occasioned by a very natural mistake. The ecclesiastical writers of the fourth or fifth centuries ascribed to the magistrates of Rome the same degree of implacable and unrelenting zeal which filled their own breasts against the heretics or the idolaters of their own times. It is not improbable that some of those persons who were raised to the dignities of the empire might have imbibed the prejudices of the populace, and that the cruel disposition of others might occasionally be stimulated by motives of avarice or of personal resentment. But it is certain, and we may appeal to the grateful confessions of the first Christians, that the greatest part of those magistrates who exercised in the provinces the authority of the emperor, or of the senate, and to whose hands alone the jurisdiction of life and death was intrusted, behaved like men of polished manners and liberal education, who respected the rules of justice, and who were conversant with the precepts of philosophy. They frequently declined the odious task of persecution, dismissed the charge with contempt, or suggested to the accused Christian some legal evasion by which he might elude the severity of the laws. Whenever they were invested with a discretionary power, they used it much less for the oppression than for the relief and benefit of the afflicted church. They were far from condemning all the Christians who were accused before their tribunal, and very far from punishing with death all those who were convicted of an obstinate adherence to the new superstition. Contenting themselves, for the most part, with the milder chastisements of imprisonment, exile, or slavery in the mines, they left the unhappy victims of their justice some reason to hope that a prosperous event, the accession, the marriage, or the triumph of an emperor might speedily restore them, by a general pardon, to their former state. The martyrs, devoted to immediate execution by the Roman magistrates, appear to have been selected from the most opposite extremes. They were either bishops and presbyters, the persons the most distinguished among the Christians by their rank and influence, and whose example might strike terror into the whole sect, or else they were the meanest and most abject among them, particularly those of the servile condition, whose lives were esteemed of little value, and whose sufferings were viewed by the ancients with too careless an indifference. The learned Origen, who from his experience as well as reading was intimately acquainted with the history of the Christians, declares in the most express terms that the number of martyrs was very

inconsiderable. His authority would alone be sufficient to annihilate that formidable army of martyrs
whose relics, drawn for the most part from the cata-
combs of Rome, have replenished so many churches,
and whose marvellous achievements have been the
subject of so many volumes of holy romance. But the
general assertion of Origen may be explained and
confirmed by the particular testimony of his friend
Dionysius, who, in the immense city of Alexandria,
and under the rigorous persecution of Decius, reckons
only ten men and seven women who suffered for the
profession of the Christian name.

During the same period of persecution, the zealous,
the eloquent, the ambitious Cyprian governed the
church, not only of Carthage, but even of Africa. He
possessed every quality which could engage the
reverence of the faithful or provoke the suspicions
and resentment of the Pagan magistrates. His
character as well as his station seemed to mark out
that holy prelate as the most distinguished object of
envy and of danger. The experience, however, of the
life of Cyprian is sufficient to prove that our fancy has
exaggerated the perilous situation of a Christian
bishop; and that the dangers to which he was exposed
were less imminent than those which temporal
ambition is always prepared to encounter in the
pursuit of honours. Four Roman emperors, with
their families, their favourites, and their adherents,
perished by the sword in the space of ten years, during
which the bishop of Carthage guided by his authority
and eloquence the counsels of the African church.
It was only in the third year of his administration
that he had reason, during a few months, to apprehend
the severe edicts of Decius, the vigilance of the magistrate, and the clamours of the multitude, who loudly
demanded that Cyprian, the leader of the Christians,
should be thrown to the lions. Prudence suggested
the necessity of a temporary retreat, and the voice of
prudence was obeyed. He withdrew himself into an
obscure solitude, from whence he could maintain a
constant correspondence with the clergy and people

of Carthage; and, concealing himself till the tempest was past, he preserved his life, without relinquishing either his power or his reputation. His extreme caution did not, however, escape the censure of the more rigid Christians who lamented, or the reproaches of his personal enemies who insulted, a conduct which they considered as a pusillanimous and criminal desertion of the most sacred duty. The propriety of reserving himself for the future exigencies of the church, the example of several holy bishops, and the divine admonitions which, as he declares himself, he frequently received in visions and ecstacies, were the reasons alleged in his justification. But his best apology may be found in the cheerful resolution with which, about eight years afterwards, he suffered death in the cause of religion. The authentic history of his martyrdom has been recorded with unusual candour and impartiality. A short abstract, therefore, of its most important circumstances will convey the clearest information of the spirit, and of the forms, of the Roman persecutions.

When Valerian was consul for the third, and Gallienus for the fourth time, Paternus, proconsul of Africa, summoned Cyprian to appear in his private council-chamber. He there acquainted him with the Imperial mandate which he had just received, that those who had abandoned the Roman religion should immediately return to the practice of the ceremonies of their ancestors. Cyprian replied without hesitation that he was a Christian and a bishop, devoted to the worship of the true and only Deity, to whom he offered up his daily supplications for the safety and prosperity of the two emperors, his lawful sovereigns. With modest confidence he pleaded the privilege of a citizen, in refusing to give any answer to some invidious and indeed illegal questions which the proconsul had proposed. A sentence of banishment was pronounced as the penalty of Cyprian's disobedience; and he was conducted, without delay, to Curubis, a free and maritime city of Zeugitana, in a pleasant situation, a fertile territory, and at the dis-

tance of about forty miles from Carthage. The
exiled bishop enjoyed the conveniencies of life and
the consciousness of virtue. His reputation was
diffused over Africa and Italy; an account of his
behaviour was published for the edification of the
Christian world; and his solitude was frequently
interrupted by the letters, the visits, and the con-
gratulations of the faithful. On the arrival of a new
proconsul in the province, the fortune of Cyprian
appeared for some time to wear a still more favourable
aspect. He was recalled from banishment; and,
though not yet permitted to return to Carthage, his
own gardens in the neighbourhood of the capital
were assigned for the place of his residence.

At length, exactly one year after Cyprian was first
apprehended, Galerius Maximus, proconsul of Africa,
received the Imperial warrant for the execution of
the Christian teachers. The bishop of Carthage was
sensible that he should be singled out for one of the
first victims; and the frailty of nature tempted him
to withdraw himself, by a secret flight, from the
danger and the honour of martyrdom; but, soon re-
covering that fortitude which his character required,
he returned to his gardens, and patiently expected
the ministers of death. Two officers of rank, who
were intrusted with that commission, placed Cyprian
between them in a chariot; and, as the proconsul was
not then at leisure, they conducted him, not to a
prison, but to a private house in Carthage, which belonged to one of them. An elegant supper was provided for the entertainment of the bishop, and his
Christian friends were permitted for the last time to
enjoy his society, whilst the streets were filled with a
multitude of the faithful, anxious and alarmed at the
approaching fate of their spiritual father. In the
morning he appeared before the tribunal of the proconsul, who, after informing himself of the name and
situation of Cyprian, commanded him to offer sacrifice,
and pressed him to reflect on the consequences of his
disobedience. The refusal of Cyprian was firm and
decisive; and the magistrate, when he had taken the

opinion of his council, pronounced with some reluctance the sentence of death. It was conceived in
the following terms : " That Thascius Cyprianus
should be immediately beheaded, as the enemy of the
gods of Rome, and as the chief and ringleader of a
criminal association, which he had seduced into an
impious resistance against the laws of the most holy
emperors, Valerian and Gallienus." The manner of
his execution was the mildest and least painful that
could be inflicted on a person convicted of any capital
offence : nor was the use of torture admitted to obtain
from the bishop of Carthage either the recantation of
his principles or the discovery of his accomplices.

As soon as the sentence was proclaimed, a general
cry of " We will die with him " arose at once among
the listening multitude of Christians who waited before the palace gates. The generous effusions of their
zeal and affection were neither serviceable to Cyprian
nor dangerous to themselves. He was led away under
a guard of tribunes and centurions, without resistance
and without insult, to the place of his execution, a
spacious and level plain near the city, which was
already filled with great numbers of spectators. His
faithful presbyters and deacons were permitted to
accompany their holy bishop. They assisted him in
laying aside his upper garment, spread linen on the
ground to catch the precious relics of his blood, and
received his orders to bestow five-and-twenty pieces
of gold on the executioner. The martyr then covered
his face with his hands, and at one blow his head was
separated from his body. His corpse remained during
some hours exposed to the curiosity of the Gentiles;
but in the night it was removed, and transported in a
triumphal procession and with a splendid illumination
to the burial-place of the Christians. The funeral of
Cyprian was publicly celebrated without receiving
any interruption from the Roman magistrates; and
those among the faithful who had performed the last
offices to his person and his memory were secure from
the danger of inquiry or of punishment. It is remarkable that of so great a multitude of bishops in the

province of Africa Cyprian was the first who was esteemed worthy to obtain the crown of martyrdom.

It was in the choice of Cyprian either to die a martyr or to live an apostate, but on that choice depended the alternative of honour or infamy. Could we suppose that the bishop of Carthage had employed the profession of the Christian faith only as the instrument of his avarice or ambition, it was still incumbent on him to support the character which he had assumed, and, if he possessed the smallest degree of manly fortitude, rather to expose himself to the most cruel tortures than by a single act to exchange the reputation of a whole life for the abhorrence of his Christian brethren and the contempt of the Gentile world. But, if the zeal of Cyprian was supported by the sincere conviction of the truth of those doctrines which he preached, the crown of martyrdom must have appeared to him as an object of desire rather than of terror. It is not easy to extract any distinct ideas from the vague though eloquent declamations of the Fathers or to ascertain the degree of immortal glory and happiness which they confidently promised to those who were so fortunate as to shed their blood in the cause of religion. They inculcated with becoming diligence that the fire of martyrdom supplied every defect and expiated every sin; that, while the souls of ordinary Christians were obliged to pass through a slow and painful purification, the triumphant sufferers entered into the immediate fruition of eternal bliss, where, in the society of the patriarchs, the apostles, and the prophets, they reigned with Christ, and acted as his assessors in the universal judgment of mankind. The assurance of a lasting reputation upon earth, a motive so congenial to the vanity of human nature, often served to animate the courage of the martyrs. The honours which Rome or Athens bestowed on those citizens who had fallen in the cause of their country were cold and unmeaning demonstrations of respect, when compared with the ardent gratitude and devotion which the primitive church expressed towards the victorious champions of the faith. The annual commemoration of their virtues and sufferings was observed as a sacred ceremony, and at length terminated in religious worship. Among the Christians who had publicly confessed their religious principles, those who (as it very frequently happened) had been dismissed from the tribunal or the prisons of the Pagan magistrates obtained such honours as were justly due to their imperfect martyrdom and their generous resolution. The most pious females courted the permission of imprinting kisses on the fetters which they had worn and on the wounds which they had received. Their persons were esteemed holy, their decisions were admitted with deference, and they too often abused, by their spiritual pride and licentious manners, the pre-eminence which their zeal and intrepidity had acquired. Distinctions like these, whilst they display the exalted merit, betray the inconsiderable number, of those who suffered and of those who died for the profession of Christianity.

The sober discretion of the present age will more readily censure than admire, but can more easily admire than imitate, the fervour of the first Christians; who, according to the lively expression of Sulpicius Severus, desired martyrdom with more eagerness than his own contemporaries solicited a bishopric. The epistles which Ignatius composed as he was carried in chains through the cities of Asia breathe sentiments the most repugnant to the ordinary feelings of human nature. He earnestly beseeches the Romans that, when he should be exposed in the amphitheatre, they would not, by their kind but unseasonable intercession, deprive him of the crown of glory; and he declares his resolution to provoke and irritate the wild beasts which might be employed as the instruments of his death. Some stories are related of the courage of martyrs who actually performed what Ignatius had intended; who exasperated the fury of the lions, pressed the executioner to hasten his office, cheerfully leaped into the fires which were kindled to consume them, and discovered a sensation of joy and pleasure in the midst of the most exquisite tortures. Several examples have been preserved of a zeal impatient of those restraints which the emperors had provided for the security of the church. The Christians sometimes supplied by their voluntary declaration the want of an accuser, rudely disturbed the public service of Paganism, and, rushing in crowds round the tribunal of the magistrates, called upon them to pronounce and to inflict the sentence of the law. The behaviour of the Christians was too remarkable to escape the notice of the ancient philosophers; but they seem to have considered it with much less admiration than astonishment. Incapable of conceiving the motives which sometimes transported the fortitude of believers beyond the bounds of prudence or reason, they treated such an eagerness to die as the strange result of obstinate despair, of stupid insensibility, or of superstitious frenzy. " Unhappy men ! " exclaimed the proconsul Antoninus to the Christians of Asia; " unhappy men ! if you are thus weary of your lives, is it so difficult for you to find ropes and precipices? " He was extremely cautious (as it is observed by a learned and pious historian) of punishing men who had found no accusers but themselves, the Imperial laws not having made any provision for so unexpected a case; condemning, therefore, a few as a warning to their brethren, he dismissed the multitude with indignation and contempt. Notwithstanding this real or affected disdain, the intrepid constancy of the faithful was productive of more salutary effects on those minds which nature or grace had disposed for the easy reception of religious truth. On these melancholy occasions, there were many among the Gentiles who pitied, who admired, and who were converted. The generous enthusiasm was communicated from the sufferer to the spectators; and the blood of martyrs, according to a well-known observation, became the seed of the church.

But, although devotion had raised, and eloquence continued to inflame, this fever of the mind, it insensibly gave way to the more natural hopes and fears of the human heart, to the love of life, the apprehension of pain, and the horror of dissolution. The more prudent rulers of the church found themselves obliged to restrain the indiscreet ardour of their followers, and to distrust a constancy which too often abandoned them in the hour of trial. As the lives of the faithful became less mortified and austere, they were every day less ambitious of the honours of martyrdom; and the soldiers of Christ, instead of distinguishing themselves by voluntary deeds of heroism, frequently deserted their post, and fled in confusion before the enemy whom it was their duty to resist. There were three methods, however, of escaping the flames of persecution, which were not attended with an equal degree of guilt : the first, indeed, was generally allowed to be innocent; the second was of a doubtful, or at least of a venial, nature; but the third implied a direct and criminal apostacy from the Christian faith.

I. A modern inquisitor would hear with surprise that, whenever an information was given to a Roman magistrate of any person within his jurisdiction who had embraced the sect of the Christians, the charge was communicated to the party accused, and that a convenient time was allowed him to settle his domestic concerns and to prepare an answer to the crime which was imputed to him. If he entertained any doubt of his own constancy, such a delay afforded him the opportunity of preserving his life and honour by flight, of withdrawing himself into some obscure retirement or some distant province, and of patiently expecting the return of peace and security. A measure so consonant to reason was soon authorized by the advice and example of the most holy prelates, and seems to have been censured by few, except by the Montanists, who deviated into heresy by their strict and obstinate adherence to the rigour of ancient discipline. II. The provincial governors, whose zeal was less prevalent than their avarice, had countenanced the practice of selling certificates (or libels as they were called), which attested that the persons therein mentioned had complied with the laws and sacrificed to the Roman deities. By producing these false declarations, the opulent and timid Christians were enabled to silence the malice of an informer and to reconcile, in some measure, their safety with their religion. A slight penance atoned for this profane dissimulation. III. In every persecution there were great numbers of unworthy Christians who publicly disowned or renounced the faith which they had professed; and who confirmed the sincerity of their abjuration by the legal acts of burning incense or of offering sacrifices. Some of these apostates had yielded on the first menace or exhortation of the magistrate; whilst the patience of others had been subdued by the length and repetition of tortures. The affrighted countenances of some betrayed their inward remorse, while others advanced, with confidence and alacrity, to the altars of the gods. But the disguise which fear had imposed subsisted no longer than the present danger. As soon as the severity of the persecution was abated, the doors of the churches were assailed by the returning multitude of penitents, who detested their idolatrous submission, and who solicited, with equal ardour, but with various success, their readmission into the society of Christians.

IV. Notwithstanding the general rules established for the conviction and punishment of the Christians, the fate of those sectaries, in an extensive and arbitrary government, must still, in a great measure, have depended on their own behaviour, the circumstances of the times, and the temper of their supreme as well as subordinate rulers. Zeal might sometimes provoke, and prudence might sometimes avert or assuage, the superstitious fury of the Pagans. A variety of motives might dispose the provincial governors either to enforce or to relax the execution of the laws; and of these motives the most forcible was their regard not only for the public edicts, but for the secret intentions of the emperor, a glance from whose eye was sufficient to kindle or to extinguish the flames of persecution. As often as any occasional severities were exercised in the different parts of the empire, the primitive Christians lamented and perhaps magnified their own sufferings; but the celebrated number of *ten* persecutions has been determined by the ecclesiastical writers of the fifth century, who possessed a more distinct view of the prosperous or adverse fortunes of the church, from the age of Nero to that of Diocletian. The ingenious parallels of the *ten* plagues of Egypt and of the *ten* horns of the Apocalypse first suggested this calculation to their minds; and in their application of the faith of prophecy to the truth of history they were careful to select those reigns which were indeed the most hostile to the Christian cause. But these transient persecutions served only to revive the zeal, and to restore the discipline, of the faithful: and the moments of extraordinary rigour were compensated by much longer intervals of peace and security. The indifference of some princes and the indulgence of others permitted the Christians to enjoy, though not perhaps a legal, yet an actual and public, toleration of their religion.

The apology of Tertullian contains two very ancient, very singular, but at the same time very suspicious, instances of Imperial clemency: the edicts published by Tiberius and by Marcus Antoninus, and designed not only to protect the innocence of the Christians, but even to proclaim those stupendous miracles which had attested the truth of their doctrine. The first of these examples is attended with some difficulties which might perplex the sceptical mind. We are required to believe *that* Pontius Pilate informed the emperor of the unjust sentence of death which he had pronounced against an innocent, and, as it appeared, a divine, person; and that, without acquiring the merit, he exposed himself to the danger, of martyrdom; *that* Tiberius, who avowed his contempt for all religion, immediately conceived the design of placing the Jewish Messiah among the gods of Rome; *that* his servile senate ventured to disobey the commands of their master; *that* Tiberius, instead of resenting their refusal, contented himself with protecting the Christians from the severity of the laws, many years before such laws were enacted, or before the church had assumed any distinct name or existence; and lastly, *that* the memory of this extraordinary transaction was preserved in the most public and authentic records, which escaped the knowledge of the historians of Greece and Rome, and were only visible to the eyes of an African Christian, who composed his apology one hundred and sixty years after the death of Tiberius. The edict of Marcus Antoninus is supposed to have been the effect of his devotion and gratitude for the miraculous deliverance which he had obtained in the Marcomannic war. The distress of the legions, the seasonable tempest of rain and hail, of thunder and lightning, and the dismay and defeat of the barbarians, have been celebrated by the eloquence of several Pagan writers. If there were any Christians in that army, it was natural that they should ascribe some merit to the fervent prayers which, in the moment of danger, they had offered up for their own and the public safety. But we are still assured by monuments of brass and marble, by the Imperial medals, and by the Antonine column, that neither the prince nor the people entertained any sense of this signal obligation, since they unanimously attribute their deliverance to the providence of Jupiter and to the interposition of Mercury. During the whole course of his reign, Marcus despised the Christians as a philosopher, and punished them as a sovereign.

By a singular fatality, the hardships which they had endured under the government of a virtuous prince immediately ceased on the accession of a tyrant, and, as none except themselves had experienced the injustice of Marcus, so they alone were protected by the lenity of Commodus. The celebrated Marcia, the most favoured of his concubines, and who at length contrived the murder of her Imperial lover, entertained a singular affection for the oppressed church; and, though it was impossible that she could reconcile the practice of vice with the precepts of the Gospel, she might hope to atone for the frailties of her sex and profession by declaring herself the patroness of the Christians. Under the gracious protection of Marcia, they passed in safety the thirteen years of a cruel tyranny; and, when the empire was established in the house of Severus, they formed a domestic but more honourable connexion with the new court. The emperor was persuaded that, in a dangerous sickness, he had derived some benefit, either spiritual or physical, from the holy oil with which one of his slaves had anointed him. He always treated with peculiar distinction several persons of both sexes who had embraced the new religion. The nurse as well as the preceptor of Caracalla were Christians; and, if that young prince ever betrayed a sentiment of humanity, it was occasioned by an incident which, however trifling, bore some relation to the cause of Christianity. Under the reign of Severus, the fury of the populace was checked; the rigour of ancient laws was for some time suspended; and the provincial governors were satisfied with receiving an annual present from the churches within their jurisdiction, as the price, or as the reward, of their moderation. The controversy concerning the precise time of the celebration of Easter armed the bishops of Asia and Italy against each other, and was considered as the most important business of this period of leisure and tranquillity. Nor was the peace of the church interrupted till the increasing numbers of proselytes seem at length to have attracted the attention, and to have alienated the mind, of Severus. With the design of restraining the progress of Christianity, he published an edict which, though it was designed to affect only the new converts, could not be carried into strict execution without exposing to danger and punishment the most zealous of their teachers and missionaries. In this mitigated persecution, we may still discover the indulgent spirit of Rome and of Polytheism, which so readily admitted every excuse in favour of those who practised the religious ceremonies of their fathers.

But the laws which Severus had enacted soon expired with the authority of that emperor; and the Christians, after this accidental tempest, enjoyed a calm of thirty-eight years. Till this period they had usually held their assemblies in private houses and sequestered places. They were now permitted to erect and consecrate convenient edifices for the purpose of religious worship; to purchase lands, even at Rome itself, for the use of the community; and to conduct the elections of their ecclesiastical ministers in so public but at the same time in so exemplary a manner as to deserve the respectful attention of the Gentiles. This long repose of the church was accompanied with dignity. The reigns of those princes who derived their extraction from the Asiatic provinces proved the most favourable to the Christians; the eminent persons of the sect, instead of being reduced to implore the protection of a slave or concubine, were admitted into the palace in the honourable characters of priests and philosophers; and their mysterious doctrines, which were already diffused among the people, insensibly attracted the curiosity of their sovereign. When the empress Mammæa passed through Antioch, she expressed a desire of conversing with the celebrated Origen, the fame of whose piety and learning was spread over the East. Origen obeyed so flattering an invitation, and, though he could not expect to succeed in the conversion of an artful and ambitious woman, she listened with pleasure to his eloquent exhortations, and honourably dismissed him to his retirement in Palestine. The sentiments of Mammæa were adopted by her son Alexander, and the philosophic devotion of that emperor was marked by a singular but injudicious regard for the Christian religion. In his domestic chapel he placed the statues of Abraham, of Orpheus, of Apollonius, and of Christ, as an honour justly due to those respectable sages who had instructed mankind in the various modes of addressing their homage to the supreme and universal deity. A purer faith, as well as worship, was openly professed and practised

among his household. Bishops, perhaps for the first
time, were seen at court; and after the death of
Alexander, when the inhuman Maximin discharged
his fury on the favourites and servants of his unfortunate benefactor, a great number of Christians, of
every rank, and of both sexes, were involved in the
promiscuous massacre, which, on their account, has
improperly received the name of Persecution.

Notwithstanding the cruel disposition of Maximin,
the effects of his resentment against the Christians
were of a very local and temporary nature, and the
pious Origen, who had been proscribed as a devoted
victim, was still reserved to convey the truths of the
Gospel to the ear of monarchs. He addressed several
edifying letters to the emperor Philip, to his wife, and
to his mother; and, as soon as that prince, who was
born in the neighbourhood of Palestine, had usurped
the Imperial sceptre, the Christians acquired a friend
and a protector. The public and even partial favour
of Philip towards the sectaries of the new religion,
and his constant reverence for the ministers of the
church, gave some colour to the suspicion, which
prevailed in his own times, that the emperor himself
was become a convert to the faith; and afforded some
grounds for a fable which was afterwards invented,
that he had been purified by confession and penance
from the guilt contracted by the murder of his innocent
predecessor. The fall of Philip introduced, with the
change of masters, a new system of government, so
oppressive to the Christians that their former condition, ever since the time of Domitian, was represented
as a state of perfect freedom and security, if compared
with the rigorous treatment which they experienced
under the short reign of Decius. The virtues of that
prince will scarcely allow us to suspect that he was
actuated by a mean resentment against the favourites
of his predecessor, and it is more reasonable to believe
that, in the prosecution of his general design to restore
the purity of Roman manners, he was desirous of
delivering the empire from what he condemned as a
recent and criminal superstition. The bishops of the

most considerable cities were removed by exile or
death; the vigilance of the magistrates prevented the
clergy of Rome during sixteen months from proceeding to a new election; and it was the opinion of
the Christians that the emperor would more patiently
endure a competitor for the purple than a bishop in
the capital. Were it possible to suppose that the
penetration of Decius had discovered pride under the
disguise of humility, or that he could foresee the
temporal dominion which might insensibly arise from
the claims of spiritual authority, we might be less
surprised that he should consider the successors of
St. Peter as the most formidable rivals to those of
Augustus.

The administration of Valerian was distinguished
by a levity and inconstancy ill-suited to the gravity
of the *Roman Censor*. In the first part of his reign,
he surpassed in clemency those princes who had been
suspected of an attachment to the Christian faith.
In the last three years and a half, listening to the
insinuations of a minister addicted to the superstitions of Egypt, he adopted the maxims, and
imitated the severity, of his predecessor Decius.
The accession of Gallienus, which increased the
calamities of the empire, restored peace to the church;
and the Christians obtained the free exercise of their
religion, by an edict addressed to the bishops and
conceived in such terms as seemed to acknowledge
their office and public character. The ancient laws,
without being formally repealed, were suffered to
sink into oblivion; and (excepting only some hostile
intentions which are attributed to the emperor
Aurelian) the disciples of Christ passed above forty
years in a state of prosperity, far more dangerous to
their virtue than the severest trials of persecution.

The story of Paul of Samosata, who filled the
metropolitan see of Antioch while the East was in
the hands of Odenathus and Zenobia, may serve to
illustrate the condition and character of the times.
The wealth of that prelate was a sufficient evidence
of his guilt, since it was neither derived from the

inheritance of his fathers nor acquired by the arts of honest industry. But Paul considered the service of the church as a very lucrative profession. His ecclesiastical jurisdiction was venal and rapacious; he extorted frequent contributions from the most opulent of the faithful, and converted to his own use a considerable part of the public revenue. By his pride and luxury the Christian religion was rendered odious in the eyes of the Gentiles. His council chamber and his throne, the splendour with which he appeared in public, the suppliant crowd who solicited his attention, the multitude of letters and petitions to which he dictated his answers, and the perpetual hurry of business in which he was involved, were circumstances much better suited to the state of a civil magistrate than to the humility of a primitive bishop. When he harangued his people from the pulpit, Paul affected the figurative style and the theatrical gestures of an Asiatic sophist, while the cathedral resounded with the loudest and most extravagant acclamations in the praise of his divine eloquence. Against those who resisted his power, or refused to flatter his vanity, the prelate of Antioch was arrogant, rigid, and inexorable; but he relaxed the discipline, and lavished the treasures, of the church on his dependent clergy, who were permitted to imitate their master in the gratification of every sensual appetite. For Paul indulged himself very freely in the pleasures of the table, and he had received into the episcopal palace two young and beautiful women, as the constant companions of his leisure moments.

Notwithstanding these scandalous vices, if Paul of Samosata had preserved the purity of the orthodox faith, his reign over the capital of Syria would have ended only with his life; and, had a seasonable persecution intervened, an effort of courage might perhaps have placed him in the rank of saints and martyrs. Some nice and subtle errors, which he imprudently adopted and obstinately maintained, concerning the doctrine of the Trinity, excited the zeal and indigna-

tion of the eastern churches. From Egypt to the
Euxine sea, the bishops were in arms and in motion.
Several councils were held, confutations were published, excommunications were pronounced, ambiguous
explanations were by turns accepted and refused,
treaties were concluded and violated, and, at length,
Paul of Samosata was degraded from his episcopal
character, by the sentence of seventy or eighty bishops,
who assembled for that purpose at Antioch, and who,
without consulting the rights of the clergy or people,
appointed a successor by their own authority. The
manifest irregularity of this proceeding increased the
numbers of the discontented faction; and as Paul,
who was no stranger to the arts of courts, had
insinuated himself into the favour of Zenobia, he
maintained above four years the possession of the
episcopal house and office. The victory of Aurelian
changed the face of the East, and the two contending
parties, who applied to each other the epithets of
schism and heresy, were either commanded or permitted to plead their cause before the tribunal of the
conqueror. This public and very singular trial affords
a convincing proof that the existence, the property,
the privileges, and the internal policy of the Christians
were acknowledged, if not by the laws, at least by
the magistrates, of the empire. As a Pagan and as a
soldier, it could scarcely be expected that Aurelian
should enter into the discussion, whether the sentiments of Paul or those of his adversaries were most
agreeable to the true standard of the orthodox faith.
His determination, however, was founded on the
general principles of equity and reason. He considered the bishops of Italy as the most impartial and
respectable judges among the Christians, and, as soon
as he was informed that they had unanimously
approved the sentence of the council, he acquiesced
in their opinion, and immediately gave orders that
Paul should be compelled to relinquish the temporal
possessions belonging to an office of which, in the
judgment of his brethren, he had been regularly
deprived. But, while we applaud the justice, we

should not overlook the policy, of Aurelian, who was desirous of restoring and cementing the dependence of the provinces on the capital by every means which could bind the interest or prejudices of any part of his subjects.

Amidst the frequent revolutions of the empire, the Christians still flourished in peace and prosperity; and, notwithstanding a celebrated æra of martyrs has been deduced from the accession of Diocletian, the new system of policy, introduced and maintained by the wisdom of that prince, continued during more than eighteen years to breathe the mildest and most liberal spirit of religious toleration. The mind of Diocletian himself was less adapted indeed to speculative inquiries than to the active labours of war and government. His prudence rendered him averse to any great innovation, and, though his temper was not very susceptible of zeal or enthusiasm, he always maintained an habitual regard for the ancient deities of the empire. But the leisure of the two empresses, of his wife Prisca and of Valeria his daughter, permitted them to listen with more attention and respect to the truths of Christianity, which in every age has acknowledged its important obligations to female devotion. The principal eunuchs, Lucian and Dorotheus, Gorgonius and Andrew, who attended the person, possessed the favour, and governed the household of Diocletian, protected by their powerful influence the faith which they had embraced. Their example was imitated by many of the most considerable officers of the palace, who in their respective stations had the care of the Imperial ornaments, of the robes, of the furniture, of the jewels, and even of the private treasury; and, though it might sometimes be incumbent on them to accompany the emperor when he sacrificed in the temple, they enjoyed, with their wives, their children, and their slaves, the free exercise of the Christian religion. Diocletian and his colleagues frequently conferred the most important offices on those persons who avowed their abhorrence for the worship of the gods, but who had displayed abilities proper for the service of the state. The bishops held an honourable rank in their respective provinces, and were treated with distinction and respect, not only by the people but by the magistrates themselves. Almost in every city, the ancient churches were found insufficient to contain the increasing multitude of proselytes; and in their place more stately and capacious edifices were erected for the public worship of the faithful. The corruption of manners and principles, so forcibly lamented by Eusebius, may be considered, not only as a consequence, but as a proof, of the liberty which the Christians enjoyed and abused under the reign of Diocletian. Prosperity had relaxed the nerves of discipline. Fraud, envy, and malice prevailed in every congregation. The presbyters aspired to the episcopal office, which every day became an object more worthy of their ambition. The bishops, who contended with each other for ecclesiastical pre-eminence, appeared by their conduct to claim a secular and tyrannical power in the church; and the lively faith which still distinguished the Christians from the Gentiles was shewn much less in their lives than in their controversial writings.

Notwithstanding this seeming security, an attentive observer might discern some symptoms that threatened the church with a more violent persecution than any which she had yet endured. The zeal and rapid progress of the Christians awakened the Polytheists from their supine indifference in the cause of those deities whom custom and education had taught them to revere. The mutual provocations of a religious war, which had already continued above two hundred years, exasperated the animosity of the contending parties. The Pagans were incensed at the rashness of a recent and obscure sect which presumed to accuse their countrymen of error and to devote their ancestors to eternal misery. The habits of justifying the popular mythology against the invectives of an implacable enemy produced in their minds some sentiments of faith and reverence for a system which they had been accustomed to consider with the most careless levity. The supernatural powers assumed by the church inspired at the same time terror and emulation. The followers of the established religion intrenched themselves behind a similar fortification of prodigies; invented new modes of sacrifice, of expiation, and of initiation; attempted to revive the credit of their expiring oracles; and listened with eager credulity to every impostor who flattered their prejudices by a tale of wonders. Both parties seemed to acknowledge the truth of those miracles which were claimed by their adversaries; and, while they were contented with ascribing them to the arts of magic and to the power of dæmons, they mutually concurred in restoring and establishing the reign of superstition. Philosophy, her most dangerous enemy, was now converted into her most useful ally. The groves of the academy, the gardens of Epicurus, and even the portico of the Stoics, were almost deserted, as so many different schools of scepticism or impiety; and many among the Romans were desirous that the writings of Cicero should be condemned and suppressed by the authority of the senate. The prevailing sect of the new Platonicians judged it prudent to connect themselves with the priests, whom perhaps they despised, against the Christians, whom they had reason to fear. These fashionable philosophers prosecuted the design of extracting allegorical wisdom from the fictions of the Greek poets; instituted mysterious rites of devotion for the use of their chosen disciples; recommended the worship of the ancient gods as the emblems or ministers of the Supreme Deity, and composed against the faith of the Gospel many elaborate treatises, which have since been committed to the flames by the prudence of orthodox emperors.

Although the policy of Diocletian and the humanity of Constantius inclined them to preserve inviolate the maxims of toleration, it was soon discovered that their two associates Maximian and Galerius entertained the most implacable aversion for the name and religion

of the Christians. The minds of those princes had
never been enlightened by science; education had
never softened their temper. They owed their greatness to their swords, and in their most elevated fortune
they still retained their superstitious prejudices of
soldiers and peasants. In the general administration
of the provinces they obeyed the laws which their
benefactor had established; but they frequently found
occasions of exercising within their camp and palaces a
secret persecution, for which the imprudent zeal of the
Christians sometimes offered the most specious pre-
tences. A sentence of death was executed upon
Maximilianus, an African youth, who had been produced by his own father before the magistrate as a
sufficient and legal recruit, but who obstinately persisted in declaring that his conscience would not permit
him to embrace the profession of a soldier. It could
scarcely be expected that any government should
suffer the action of Marcellus the centurion to pass with
impunity. On the day of a public festival, that officer
threw away his belt, his arms, and the ensigns of his
office, and exclaimed with a loud voice that he would
obey none but Jesus Christ the eternal King, and that
he renounced for ever the use of carnal weapons and
the service of an idolatrous master. The soldiers, as
soon as they recovered from their astonishment,
secured the person of Marcellus. He was examined in
the city of Tingi by the president of that part of
Mauritania; and, as he was convicted by his own confession, he was condemned and beheaded for the crime
of desertion. Examples of such a nature savour much
less of religious persecution than of martial or even
civil law ; but they served to alienate the mind of the
emperors, to justify the severity of Galerius, who dismissed a great number of Christian officers from their
employments, and to authorize the opinion that a sect
of enthusiasts which avowed principles so repugnant
to the public safety must either remain useless, or
would soon become dangerous, subjects of the empire.

After the success of the Persian war had raised the
hopes and the reputation of Galerius, he passed a

winter with Diocletian in the palace of Nicomedia; and the fate of Christianity became the object of their secret consultations. The experienced emperor was still inclined to pursue measures of lenity; and, though he readily consented to exclude the Christians from holding any employments in the household or the army, he urged in the strongest terms the danger as well as cruelty of shedding the blood of those deluded fanatics. Galerius at length extorted from him the permission of summoning a council, composed of a few persons the most distinguished in the civil and military departments of the state. The important question was agitated in their presence, and those ambitious courtiers easily discerned that it was incumbent on them to second, by their eloquence, the importunate violence of the Cæsar. It may be presumed that they insisted on every topic which might interest the pride, the piety, or the fears, of their sovereign in the destruction of Christianity. Perhaps they represented that the glorious work of the deliverance of the empire was left imperfect, as long as an independent people was permitted to subsist and multiply in the heart of the provinces. The Christians (it might speciously be alleged), renouncing the gods and the institutions of Rome, had constituted a distinct republic, which might yet be suppressed before it had acquired any military force; but which was already governed by its own laws and magistrates, was possessed of a public treasure, and was intimately connected in all its parts by the frequent assemblies of the bishops, to whose decrees their numerous and opulent congregations yielded an implicit obedience. Arguments like these may seem to have determined the reluctant mind of Diocletian to embrace a new system of persecution: but though we may suspect, it is not in our power to relate, the secret intrigues of the palace, the private views and resentments, the jealousy of women or eunuchs, and all those trifling but decisive causes which so often influence the fate of empires and the councils of the wisest monarchs.

The pleasure of the emperors was at length signified

to the Christians, who, during the course of this melancholy winter, had expected with anxiety the result of so many secret consultations. The twenty-third of February, which coincided with the Roman festival of the Terminalia, was appointed (whether from accident or design) to set bounds to the progress of Christianity. At the earliest dawn of day, the Prætorian præfect, accompanied by several generals, tribunes, and officers of the revenue, repaired to the principal church of Nicomedia, which was situated on an eminence in the most populous and beautiful part of the city. The doors were instantly broken open; they rushed into the sanctuary; and, as they searched in vain for some visible object of worship, they were obliged to content themselves with committing to the flames the volumes of holy scripture. The ministers of Diocletian were followed by a numerous body of guards and pioneers, who marched in order of battle, and were provided with all the instruments used in the destruction of fortified cities. By their incessant labour, a sacred edifice, which towered above the Imperial palace, and had long excited the indignation and envy of the Gentiles, was in a few hours levelled with the ground.

The next day the general edict of persecution was published; and, though Diocletian, still averse to the effusion of blood, had moderated the fury of Galerius, who proposed that every one refusing to offer sacrifice should immediately be burnt alive, the penalties inflicted on the obstinacy of the Christians might be deemed sufficiently rigorous and effectual. It was enacted that their churches, in all the provinces of the empire, should be demolished to their foundations; and the punishment of death was denounced against all who should presume to hold any secret assemblies for the purpose of religious worship. The philosophers, who now assumed the unworthy office of directing the blind zeal of persecution, had diligently studied the nature and genius of the Christian religion; and, as they were not ignorant that the speculative doctrines of the faith were supposed to be contained in the writings of the prophets, of the evangelists, and of the apostles, they most probably suggested the order that the bishops and presbyters should deliver all their sacred books into the hands of the magistrates, who were commanded, under the severest penalties, to burn them in a public and solemn manner. By the same edict, the property of the church was at once confiscated; and the several parts of which it might consist were either sold to the highest bidder, united to the Imperial domain, bestowed on the cities and corporations, or granted to the solicitations of rapacious courtiers. After taking such effectual measures to abolish the worship and to dissolve the government of the Christians, it was thought necessary to subject to the most intolerable hardships the condition of those perverse individuals who should still reject the religion of Nature, of Rome, and of their ancestors. Persons of a liberal birth were declared incapable of holding any honours or employments; slaves were for ever deprived of the hopes of freedom, and the whole body of the people were put out of the protection of the law. The judges were authorized to hear and to determine every action that was brought against a Christian. But the Christians were not permitted to complain of any injury which they themselves had suffered; and thus those unfortunate sectaries were exposed to the severity, while they were excluded from the benefits, of public justice. This new species of martyrdom, so painful and lingering, so obscure and ignominious, was perhaps the most proper to weary the constancy of the faithful; nor can it be doubted that the passions and interest of mankind were disposed on this occasion to second the designs of the emperors. But the policy of a well-ordered government must sometimes have interposed in behalf of the oppressed Christians; nor was it possible for the Roman princes entirely to remove the apprehension of punishment, or to connive at every act of fraud and violence, without exposing their own authority and the rest of their subjects to the most alarming dangers.

This edict was scarcely exhibited to the public view, in the most conspicuous place of Nicomedia, before it was torn down by the hands of a Christian, who expressed, at the same time, by the bitterest invectives, his contempt as well as abhorrence for such impious and tyrannical governors. His offence, according to the mildest laws, amounted to treason, and deserved death. And, if it be true that he was a person of rank and education, those circumstances could serve only to aggravate his guilt. He was burnt, or rather roasted, by a slow fire; and his executioners, zealous to revenge the personal insult which had been offered to the emperors, exhausted every refinement of cruelty, without being able to subdue his patience, or to alter the steady and insulting smile which in his dying agonies he still preserved in his countenance. The Christians, though they confessed that his conduct had not been strictly conformable to the laws of prudence, admired the divine fervour of his zeal; and the excessive commendations which they lavished on the memory of their hero and martyr contributed to fix a deep impression of terror and hatred in the mind of Diocletian.

His fears were soon alarmed by the view of a danger from which he very narrowly escaped. Within fifteen days the palace of Nicomedia, and even the bed-chamber of Diocletian, were twice in flames; and, though both times they were extinguished without any material damage, the singular repetition of the fire was justly considered as an evident proof that it had not been the effect of chance or negligence. The suspicion naturally fell on the Christians; and it was suggested, with some degree of probability, that those desperate fanatics, provoked by their present sufferings and apprehensive of impending calamities, had entered into a conspiracy with their faithful brethren, the eunuchs of the palace, against the lives of two emperors, whom they detested as the irreconcileable enemies of the church of God. Jealousy and resentment prevailed in every breast, but especially in that of Diocletian. A great number of persons, distinguished either by the offices which they had filled or by the favour which they had enjoyed, were thrown into prison. Every mode of torture was put in practice, and the court, as well as city, was polluted with many bloody executions. But, as it was found impossible to extort any discovery of this mysterious transaction, it seems incumbent on us either to presume the innocence, or to admire the resolution, of the sufferers. A few days afterwards Galerius hastily withdrew himself from Nicomedia, declaring that, if he delayed his departure from that devoted palace, he should fall a sacrifice to the rage of the Christians. The ecclesiastical historians, from whom alone we derive a partial and imperfect knowledge of this persecution, are at a loss how to account for the fears and dangers of the emperors. Two of these writers, a Prince and a Rhetorician, were eye-witnesses of the fire of Nicomedia. The one ascribes it to lightning, and the divine wrath; the other affirms that it was kindled by the malice of Galerius himself.

As the edict against the Christians was designed for a general law of the whole empire, and as Diocletian and Galerius, though they might not wait for the consent, were assured of the concurrence, of the western princes, it would appear more consonant to our ideas of policy that the governors of all the provinces should have received secret instructions to publish, on one and the same day, this declaration of war within their respective departments. It was at least to be expected that the convenience of the public highways and established posts would have enabled the emperors to transmit their orders with the utmost dispatch from the palace of Nicomedia to the extremities of the Roman world; and that they would not have suffered fifty days to elapse before the edict was published in Syria, and near four months before it was signified to the cities of Africa. This delay may perhaps be imputed to the cautious temper of Diocletian, who had yielded a reluctant consent to the measures of persecution, and who was desirous of trying the experiment under his more immediate eye, before he gave way to the disorders and discontent which it must inevitably occasion in the distant provinces. At first, indeed, the magistrates were restrained from the effusion of blood; but the use of every other severity was permitted and even recommended to their zeal; nor could the Christians, though they cheerfully resigned the ornaments of their churches, resolve to interrupt their religious assemblies or to deliver their sacred books to the flames. The pious obstinacy of Felix, an African bishop, appears to have embarrassed the subordinate ministers of the government. The curator of his city sent him in chains to the proconsul. The proconsul transmitted him to the Prætorian præfect of Italy; and Felix, who disdained even to give an evasive answer, was at length beheaded at Venusia, in Lucania, a place on which the birth of Horace has conferred fame. This precedent, and perhaps some Imperial rescript, which was issued in consequence of it, appeared to authorize the governors of provinces in punishing with death the refusal of the Christians to deliver up their sacred books. There were undoubtedly many persons who embraced this opportunity of obtaining the crown of martyrdom; but there were likewise too many who purchased an ignominious life by discovering and betraying the holy scripture into the hands of infidels. A great number even of bishops and presbyters acquired, by this criminal compliance, the opprobrious epithet of *Traditors;* and their offence was productive of much present scandal, and of much future discord, in the African church.

The copies, as well as the versions, of scripture were already so multiplied in the empire that the most severe inquisition could no longer be attended with any fatal consequences; and even the sacrifice of those volumes which, in every congregation, were preserved for public use required the consent of some treacherous and unworthy Christians. But the ruin of the churches was easily effected by the authority of the government and by the labour of the Pagans. In some provinces, however, the magistrates contented themselves with shutting up the places of religious worship. In others, they more literally complied with the terms of the edict; and, after taking away the doors, the benches, and the pulpit, which they burnt, as it were in a funeral pile, they completely demolished the remainder of the edifice. It is perhaps to this melancholy occasion that we should apply a very remarkable story, which is related with so many circumstances of variety and improbability that it serves rather to excite than to satisfy our curiosity. In a small town in Phrygia, of whose name as well as situation we are left ignorant, it should seem that the magistrates and the body of the people had embraced the Christian faith; and, as some resistance might be apprehended to the execution of the edict, the governor of the province was supported by a numerous detachment of legionaries. On their approach the citizens threw themselves into the church, with the resolution either of defending by arms that sacred edifice or of perishing in its ruins. They indignantly rejected the notice and permission which was given them to retire, till the soldiers, provoked by their obstinate refusal, set fire to the building on all sides, and consumed, by this extraordinary kind of martyrdom, a great number of Phrygians, with their wives and children.

Some slight disturbances, though they were suppressed almost as soon as excited, in Syria and the frontiers of Armenia, afforded the enemies of the church a very plausible occasion to insinuate that those troubles had been secretly fomented by the intrigues of the bishops, who had already forgotten their ostentatious professions of passive and unlimited obedience. The resentment, or the fears, of Diocletian at length transported him beyond the bounds of moderation which he had hitherto preserved, and he declared, in a series of cruel edicts, his intention of abolishing the Christian name. By the first of these edicts, the governors of the provinces were directed to apprehend all persons of the ecclesiastical order; and the prisons, destined for the vilest criminals, were soon filled with a multitude of bishops, presbyters, deacons, readers, and exorcists. By a second edict, the magistrates were commanded to employ every method of severity which might reclaim them from their odious superstition and oblige them to return to the established worship of the gods. This rigorous order was extended by a subsequent edict to the whole body of Christians, who were exposed to a violent and general persecution. Instead of those salutary restraints, which had required the direct and solemn testimony of an accuser, it became the duty as well as the interest of the imperial officers to discover, to pursue, and to torment the most obnoxious among the faithful. Heavy penalties were denounced against all who should presume to save a proscribed sectary from the just indignation of the gods, and of the emperors. Yet, notwithstanding the severity of this law, the virtuous courage of many of the Pagans, in concealing their friends or relations, affords an honourable proof that the rage of superstition had not extinguished in their minds the sentiments of nature and humanity.

Diocletian had no sooner published his edicts against the Christians than, as if he had been desirous of committing to other hands the work of persecution, he divested himself of the Imperial purple. The character and situation of his colleagues and successors sometimes urged them to enforce, and sometimes inclined them to suspend the execution of these rigorous laws; nor can we acquire a just and distinct idea of this important period of ecclesiastical history, unless we separately consider the state of Christianity, in the different parts of the empire, during the space of ten years which elapsed between the first edicts of Diocletian and the final peace of the church.

The mild and humane temper of Constantius was averse to the oppression of any part of his subjects. The principal offices of his palace were exercised by Christians. He loved their persons, esteemed their fidelity, and entertained not any dislike to their religious principles. But, as long as Constantius remained in the subordinate station of Cæsar, it was not in his power openly to reject the edicts of Diocletian or to disobey the commands of Maximian. His authority contributed, however, to alleviate the sufferings which he pitied and abhorred. He consented, with reluctance, to the ruin of the churches; but he ventured to protect the Christians themselves from the fury of the populace and from the rigour of the laws. The provinces of Gaul (under which we may probably include those of Britain) were indebted for the singular tranquillity which they enjoyed to the gentle interposition of their sovereign. But Datianus, the president or governor of Spain, actuated either by zeal or policy, chose rather to execute the public edicts of the emperors than to understand the secret intentions of Constantius; and it can scarcely be doubted that his provincial administration was stained with the blood of a few martyrs. The elevation of Constantius to the supreme and independent dignity of Augustus gave a free scope to the exercise of his virtues, and the shortness of his reign did not prevent him from establishing a system of toleration, of which he left the precept and the example to his son Constantine. His fortunate son, from the first moment of his accession declaring himself the protector of the church, at length deserved the appellation of the first emperor who publicly professed and established the Christian religion. The motives of his conversion, as they may variously be deduced from benevolence, from policy, from conviction, or from remorse; and the progress of the revolution which, under his powerful influence, and that of his sons, rendered Christianity the reigning religion of the Roman empire, will form a very interesting and important chapter in the second volume of this history. At present it may be sufficient to observe that every victory of Constantine was productive of some relief or benefit to the church.

The provinces of Italy and Africa experienced a short but violent persecution. The rigorous edicts of Diocletian were strictly and cheerfully executed by his associate Maximian, who had long hated the Christians, and who delighted in acts of blood and violence. In the autumn of the first year of the persecution, the two emperors met at Rome to celebrate their triumph; several oppressive laws appear to have issued from their secret consultations, and the diligence of the magistrates was animated by the presence of their sovereigns. After Diocletian had divested him. self of the purple, Italy and Africa were administered under the name of Severus, and were exposed, without defence, to the implacable resentment of his master Galerius. Among the martyrs of Rome, Adauctus deserves the notice of posterity. He was of a noble family in Italy, and had raised himself, through the successive honours of the palace, to the important office of treasurer of the private demesnes. Adauctus is the more remarkable for being the only person of rank and distinction who appears to have suffered death during the whole course of this general persecution.

The revolt of Maxentius immediately restored peace to the churches of Italy and Africa; and the same tyrant who oppressed every other class of his subjects showed himself just, humane, and even partial, towards the afflicted Christians. He depended on their gratitude and affection, and very naturally presumed that the injuries which they had suffered, and the dangers which they still apprehended from his most inveterate enemy, would secure the fidelity of a party already considerable by their numbers and opulence. Even the conduct of Maxentius towards the bishops of Rome and Carthage may be considered as the proof of his toleration, since it is probable that the most orthodox princes would adopt the same measures with regard to their established clergy. Marcellus, the former of those prelates, had thrown the capital into confusion by the severe penance which he imposed on a great number of Christians, who, during the late persecution, had renounced or dissembled their religion. The rage of faction broke out in frequent and violent seditions; the blood of the faithful was shed by each other's hands; and the exile of Marcellus, whose prudence seems to have been less eminent than his zeal, was found to be the only measure capable of restoring peace to the distracted church of Rome. The behaviour of Mensurius, bishop of Carthage, appears to have been still more reprehensible. A deacon of that city had published a libel against the emperor. The offender took refuge in the episcopal palace; and, though it was somewhat early to advance any claims of ecclesiastical immunities, the bishop refused to deliver him up to the officers of justice. For this treasonable resistance, Mensurius was summoned to court, and, instead of receiving a legal sentence of death or banishment, he was permitted, after a short examination, to return to his diocese. Such was the happy condition of the Christian subjects of Maxentius that, whenever they were desirous of procuring for their own use any bodies of martyrs, they were obliged to purchase them from the most distant provinces of the East. A story is related of Aglae, a Roman lady, descended from a consular family, and possessed of so ample an estate that it required the management of seventy-three stewards. Among these, Boniface was the favourite of his mistress; and, as Aglae mixed love with devotion, it is reported that he was admitted to share her bed. Her fortune enabled her to gratify the pious desire of obtaining some sacred relics from the East. She intrusted Boniface with a considerable sum of gold and a large quantity of aromatics; and her lover, attended by twelve horsemen and three covered chariots, undertook a remote pilgrimage, as far as Tarsus in Cilicia.

The sanguinary temper of Galerius, the first and principal author of the persecution, was formidable to those Christians whom their misfortunes had placed within the limits of his dominions; and it may fairly be presumed that many persons of a middle rank, who were not confined by the chains either of wealth or of poverty, very frequently deserted their native country, and sought a refuge in the milder climate of the West. As long as he commanded only the armies and provinces of Illyricum, he could with difficulty either find or make a considerable number of martyrs, in a warlike country, which had entertained the missionaries of the Gospel with more coldness and reluctance than any other part of the empire. But, when Galerius had obtained the supreme power and the government of the East, he indulged in their fullest extent his zeal and cruelty, not only in the provinces of Thrace and Asia, which acknowledged his immediate jurisdiction, but in those of Syria, Palestine, and Egypt, where Maximin gratified his own inclination by yielding a rigorous obedience to the stern commands of his benefactor. The frequent disappointments of his ambitious views, the experience of six years of persecution, and the salutary reflections which a lingering and painful distemper suggested to the mind of Galerius, at length convinced him that the most violent efforts of despotism are insufficient to extirpate a whole people or to subdue their religious prejudices. Desirous of repairing the mischief that he had occasioned, he published in his own name, and in those of Licinius and Constantine, a general edict, which, after a pompous recital of the Imperial titles, proceeded in the following manner :

" Among the important cares which have occupied our mind for the utility and preservation of the empire, it was our intention to correct and re-establish all things according to the ancient laws and public discipline of the Romans. We were particularly desirous of reclaiming into the way of reason and nature the deluded Christians, who had renounced the religion and ceremonies instituted by their fathers, and, presumptuously despising the practice of antiquity, had invented extravagant laws and opinions, according to the dictates of their fancy, and had collected a various society from the different provinces of our empire. The edicts which we have published to enforce the worship of the gods having exposed many of the Christians to danger and distress, many having suffered death, and many more, who still persist in their impious folly, being left destitute of *any* public exercise of religion, we are disposed to extend to those unhappy men the effects of our wonted clemency. We permit them, therefore, freely to profess their private opinions, and to assemble in their conventicles without fear or molestation, provided always that they preserve a due respect to the established laws and government. By another rescript we shall signify our intentions to the judges and magistrates; and we hope that our indulgence will engage the Christians to offer up their prayers to the Deity whom they adore, for our safety and prosperity, for their own, and for that of the republic." It is not usually in the language of edicts and manifestoes that we should search for the real character or the secret motives of princes; but, as these were the words of a dying emperor, his situation, perhaps, may be admitted as a pledge of his sincerity.

When Galerius subscribed this edict of toleration, he was well assured that Licinius would readily comply with the inclinations of his friend and benefactor, and that any measures in favour of the Christians would obtain the approbation of Constantine. But the emperor would not venture to insert in the preamble the name of Maximin, whose consent was of the greatest importance, and who succeeded a few days afterwards to the provinces of Asia. In the first six months, however, of his new reign, Maximin affected to adopt the prudent counsels of his predecessor; and, though he never condescended to secure the tranquillity of the church by a public edict, Sabinus, his Prætorian præfect, addressed a circular letter to all the governors and magistrates of the provinces, expatiating on the Imperial clemency, acknowledging the invincible obstinacy of the Christians, and directing the officers of justice to cease their ineffectual prosecutions and to connive at the secret assemblies of those enthusiasts. In consequence of these orders, great numbers of Christians were released from prison or delivered from the mines. The confessors, singing hymns of triumph, returned into their own countries; and those who had yielded to the violence of the tempest solicited with tears of repentance their re-admission into the bosom of the church.

But this treacherous calm was of short duration;

nor could the Christians of the East place any confidence in the character of their sovereign. Cruelty
and superstition were the ruling passions of the soul of
Maximin.   The former suggested the means, the latter
pointed out the objects, of persecution.   The emperor
was devoted to the worship of the gods, to the study
of magic, and to the belief of oracles.   The prophets
or philosophers whom he revered as the favourites
of heaven were frequently raised to the government
of provinces and admitted into his most secret
counsels. They easily convinced him that the
Christians had been indebted for their victories to
their regular discipline, and that the weakness of
Polytheism had principally flowed from a want of
union and subordination among the ministers of
religion. A system of government was therefore
instituted, which was evidently copied from the policy
of the church.   In all the great cities of the empire,
the temples were repaired and beautified by the order
of Maximin; and the officiating priests of the various
deities were subjected to the authority of a superior
pontiff, destined to oppose the bishop and to promote
the cause of Paganism.   These pontiffs acknowledged,
in their turn, the supreme jurisdiction of the metropolitans or high priests of the province, who acted as
the immediate vicegerents of the emperor himself.   A
white robe was the ensign of their dignity; and these
new prelates were carefully selected from the most
noble and opulent families.   By the influence of the
magistrates and of the sacerdotal order, a great
number of dutiful addresses were obtained, particularly from the cities of Nicomedia, Antioch, and
Tyre, which artfully represented the well-known
intentions of the court as the general sense of the
people; solicited the emperor to consult the laws of
justice rather than the dictates of his clemency;
expressed their abhorrence of the Christians; and
humbly prayed that those impious sectaries might at
least be excluded from the limits of their respective
territories.   The answer of Maximin to the address
which he obtained from the citizens of Tyre is still

extant. He praises their zeal and devotion in terms of the highest satisfaction, descants on the obstinate impiety of the Christians, and betrays, by the readiness with which he consents to their banishment, that he considered himself as receiving, rather than as conferring, an obligation. The priests, as well as the magistrates, were empowered to enforce the execution of his edicts, which were engraved on tables of brass; and, though it was recommended to them to avoid the effusion of blood, the most cruel and ignominious punishments were inflicted on the refractory Christians.

The Asiatic Christians had everything to dread from the severity of a bigoted monarch who prepared his measures of violence with such deliberate policy. But a few months had scarcely elapsed before the edicts published by the two western emperors obliged Maximin to suspend the prosecution of his designs: the civil war, which he so rashly undertook against Licinius, employed all his attention; and the defeat and death of Maximin soon delivered the church from the last and most implacable of her enemies.

In this general view of the persecution which was first authorized by the edicts of Diocletian, I have purposely refrained from describing the particular sufferings and deaths of the Christian martyrs. It would have been an easy task, from the history of Eusebius, from the declamations of Lactantius, and from the most ancient acts, to collect a long series of horrid and disgustful pictures, and to fill many pages with racks and scourges, with iron hooks, and red-hot beds, and with all the variety of tortures which fire and steel, savage beasts and more savage executioners, could inflict on the human body. These melancholy scenes might be enlivened by a crowd of visions and miracles destined either to delay the death, to celebrate the triumph, or to discover the relics, of those canonized saints who suffered for the name of Christ. But I cannot determine what I ought to transcribe, till I am satisfied how much I ought to believe. The gravest of the ecclesiastical historians, Eusebius

himself, indirectly confesses that he has related whatever might redound to the glory, and that he has
suppressed all that could tend to the disgrace, of religion.   Such an acknowledgment will naturally excite
a suspicion that a writer who has so openly violated
one of the fundamental laws of history has not paid
a very strict regard to the observance of the other ;
and the suspicion will derive additional credit from the
character of Eusebius, which was less tinctured with
credulity, and more practised in the arts of courts,
than that of almost any of his contemporaries.   On
some particular occasions, when the magistrates were
exasperated by some personal motives of interest or
resentment, when the zeal of the martyrs urged them
to forget the rules of prudence, and perhaps of decency,
to overturn the altars, to pour out imprecations against
the emperors, or to strike the judge as he sat on his
tribunal, it may be presumed that every mode of
torture which cruelty could invent or constancy could
endure was exhausted on those devoted victims.
Two circumstances, however, have been unwarily mentioned, which insinuate that the general treatment of
the Christians who had been apprehended by the
officers of justice was less intolerable than it is usually
imagined to have been.   1. The confessors who were
condemned to work in the mines were permitted, by
the humanity or the negligence of their keepers, to
build chapels and freely to profess their religion in the
midst of those dreary habitations.   2. The bishops
were obliged to check and to censure the forward zeal
of the Christians who voluntarily threw themselves
into the hands of the magistrates.   Some of these were
persons oppressed by poverty and debts, who blindly
sought to terminate a miserable existence by a glorious
death.   Others were allured by the hope that a short
confinement would expiate the sins of a whole life ;
and others, again, were actuated by the less honourable motive of deriving a plentiful subsistence, and
perhaps a considerable profit, from the alms which
the charity of the faithful bestowed on the prisoners.·
After the church had triumphed over all her enemies,

the interest as well as vanity of the captives prompted them to magnify the merit of their respective suffering. A convenient distance of time or place gave an ample scope to the progress of fiction ; and the frequent instances which might be alleged of holy martyrs whose wounds had been instantly healed, whose strength had been renewed, and whose lost members had miraculously been restored, were extremely convenient for the purpose of removing every difficulty and of silencing every objection. The most extravagant legends, as they conduced to the honour of the church, were applauded by the credulous multitude, countenanced by the power of the clergy, and attested by the suspicious evidence of ecclesiastical history.

The vague descriptions of exile and imprisonment, of pain and torture, are so easily exaggerated or softened by the pencil of an artful orator that we are naturally induced to inquire into a fact of a more distinct and stubborn kind ; the number of persons who suffered death, in consequence of the edicts published by Diocletian, his associates, and his successors. The recent legendaries record whole armies and cities which were at once swept away by the undistinguishing rage of persecution. The more ancient writers content themselves with pouring out a liberal effusion of loose and tragical invectives, without condescending to ascertain the precise number of those persons who were permitted to seal with their blood their belief of the gospel. From the history of Eusebius, it may however be collected that only nine bishops were punished with death ; and we are assured, by his particular enumeration of the martyrs of Palestine, that no more than ninety-two Christians were entitled to that honourable appellation. As we are unacquainted with the degree of episcopal zeal and courage which prevailed at that time, it is not in our power to draw any useful inferences from the former of these facts ; but the latter may serve to justify a very important and probable conclusion. According to the distribution of Roman provinces, Palestine may be

considered as the sixteenth part of the Eastern empire;
and since there were some governors who, from a real
or affected clemency, had preserved their hands un-
stained with the blood of the faithful, it is reasonable
to believe that the country which had given birth to
Christianity produced at least the sixteenth part of
the martyrs who suffered death within the dominions
of Galerius and Maximin; the whole might consequently amount to about fifteen hundred; a number
which, if it is equally divided between the ten years
of the persecution, will allow an annual consumption
of one hundred and fifty martyrs.   Allotting the same
proportion to the provinces of Italy, Africa, and perhaps Spain, where, at the end of two or three years,
the rigour of the penal laws was either suspended or
abolished, the multitude of Christians in the Roman
empire on whom a capital punishment was inflicted
by a judicial sentence will be reduced to somewhat less
than two thousand persons.   Since it cannot be
doubted that the Christians were more numerous, and
their enemies more exasperated, in the time of
Diocletian, than they had ever been in any former
persecution, this probable and moderate computation
may teach us to estimate the number of primitive
saints and martyrs who sacrificed their lives for the
important purpose of introducing Christianity into
the world.

  We shall conclude this chapter by a melancholy
truth which obtrudes itself on the reluctant mind;
that even admitting, without hesitation or inquiry,
all that history has recorded, or devotion has feigned,
on the subject of martyrdoms, it must still be acknowledged that the Christians, in the course of their intestine dissensions, have inflicted far greater severities on
each other than they had experienced from the zeal of
infidels.   During the ages of ignorance which followed
the subversion of the Roman empire in the West, the
bishops of the Imperial city extended their dominion
over the laity as well as clergy of the Latin church.
The fabric of superstition which they had erected,
and which might long have defied the feeble efforts of

reason, was at length assaulted by a crowd of daring fanatics, who, from the twelfth to the sixteenth century, assumed the popular character of reformers. The church of Rome defended by violence the empire which she had acquired by fraud; a system of peace and benevolence was soon disgraced by proscriptions, wars, massacres, and the institution of the holy office. And, as the reformers were animated by the love of civil as well as of religious freedom, the Catholic princes connected their own interest with that of the clergy, and enforced by fire and the sword the terrors of spiritual censures. In the Netherlands alone, more than one hundred thousand of the subjects of Charles the Fifth are said to have suffered by the hand of the executioner; and this extraordinary number is attested by Grotius, a man of genius and learning, who preserved his moderation amidst the fury of contending sects, and who composed the annals of his own age and country, at a time when the invention of printing had facilitated the means of intelligence and increased the danger of detection. If we are obliged to submit our belief to the authority of Grotius, it must be allowed that the number of Protestants who were executed in a single province and a single reign far exceeded that of the primitive martyrs in the space of three centuries and of the Roman empire. But, if the improbability of the fact itself should prevail over the weight of evidence; if Grotius should be convicted of exaggerating the merit and sufferings of the Reformers; we shall be naturally led to inquire what confidence can be placed in the doubtful and imperfect monuments of ancient credulity; what degree of credit can be assigned to a courtly bishop and a passionate declaimer, who, under the protection of Constantine, enjoyed the exclusive privilege of recording the persecutions inflicted on the Christians by the vanquished rivals or disregarded predecessors of their gracious sovereign.

ORDER FORM

GREAT BOOKS IN PHILOSOPHY PAPERBACK SERIES

ETHICS

Aristotle—*The Nicomachean Ethics*	$7.95
Jeremy Bentham—*The Principles of Morals and Legislation*	7.95
Immanuel Kant—*The Fundamental Principles of the Metaphysic of Morals*	4.95
John Stuart Mill—*Utilitarianism*	4.95
George Edward Moore—*Principia Ethica*	7.95
Friedrich Nietzsche—*Beyond Good and Evil*	6.95
Bertrand Russell—*On Ethics, Sex, and Marriage* (edited by Al Seckel)	16.95
Benedict de Spinoza—*Ethics* and *The Improvement of the Understanding*	8.95

SOCIAL AND POLITICAL PHILOSOPHY

Aristotle—*The Politics*	6.95
Edmund Burke—*Reflections on the Revolution in France*	6.95
John Dewey—*Freedom and Culture*	9.95
G.W.F. Hegel—*The Philosophy of History*	8.95
Thomas Hobbes—*The Leviathan*	6.95
Sidney Hook—*Paradoxes of Freedom*	8.95
Sidney Hook—*Reason, Social Myths, and Democracy*	10.95
John Locke—*Second Treatise on Civil Government*	4.95
Niccolo Machiavelli—*The Prince*	4.95
Karl Marx/Frederick Engels—*The Economic and Philosophic Manuscripts of 1844* and *The Communist Manifesto*	5.95
John Stuart Mill—*Considerations on Representative Government*	6.95
John Stuart Mill—*On Liberty*	4.95
John Stuart Mill—*On Socialism*	6.95
John Stuart Mill—*The Subjection of Women*	4.95
Thomas Paine—*Rights of Man*	6.95
Plato—*The Republic*	7.95
Plato on Homosexuality: Lysis, Phaedrus, and *Symposium*	5.95
Jean-Jacques Rousseau—*The Social Contract*	5.95
Mary Wollstonecraft—*A Vindication of the Rights of Women*	5.95

METAPHYSICS/EPISTEMOLOGY

Aristotle—*De Anima*   5.95
Aristotle—*The Metaphysics*   8.95
George Berkeley—*Three Dialogues Between Hylas and Philonous*   4.95
René Descartes—*Discourse on Method* and *The Meditations*   5.95
David Hume—*An Enquiry Concerning Human Understanding*   4.95
William James—*Pragmatism*   6.95
Immanuel Kant—*Critique of Pure Reason*   7.95
Plato—*The Euthyphro, Apology, Crito,* and *Phaedo*   4.95
Bertrand Russell—*The Problems of Philosophy*   7.95
Sextus Empiricus—*Outlines of Pyrrhonism*   7.95

PHILOSOPHY OF RELIGION

Ludwig Feuerbach—*The Essence of Christianity*   7.95
David Hume—*Dialogues Concerning Natural Religion*   4.95
John Locke—*A Letter Concerning Toleration*   3.95
Thomas Paine—*The Age of Reason*   12.95
Bertrand Russell—*On God and Religion* (edited by Al Seckel)   16.95

GREAT MINDS PAPERBACK SERIES

Charles Darwin—*The Origin of Species*   9.95
Edward Gibbon—*On Christianity*   8.95

SPECIAL—For your library . . . the entire collection of 42 "Great Books in Philosophy" available at a savings of more than 15%. Only $250.00 (plus $9.00 postage and handling). Please indicate "Great Books—Complete Set" on your order form.

The books listed can be obtained from your book dealer or directly from Prometheus Books. Please indicate the appropriate books. Remittance must accompany all orders from individuals. Please include $3.00 postage and handling for the first book and $1.50 for each additional title (maximum $9.00. NYS residents please add applicable sales tax.) **Prices subject to change without notice.**

Send to _____
Please type or print clearly)

Address _____

City _____ State _____ Zip _____

Amount enclosed _____

Charge my ☐ **VISA** ☐ **MasterCard**

Account # [ ][ ][ ][ ][ ][ ][ ][ ][ ][ ][ ][ ][ ][ ][ ][ ]

Exp. Date _____/_____ Tel.# _____

Signature _____

Prometheus Books Editorial Offices
700 E. Amherst St., Buffalo, New York 14215

Distribution Facilities
59 John Glenn Drive, Amherst, New York 14228

Phone Orders call toll free: (800) 421-0351
FAX: (716) 691-0137
Please allow 3-6 weeks for delivery